Robbie

by

David Cookson

Based on Frank Robinson's own manuscript

Foreword by

Bert Hazell, *C.B.E., J.P., M.Univ:York*

Highgate Publications (Beverley) Ltd.
1989

Acknowledgements:

Grateful thanks are expressed to:
Humberside Libraries and Arts for permission to reproduce the photograph of Patrington church (on the front cover) from the illustrations collection at Beverley Library, and the photograph, 'Sports, Tientsin' (page 20) and the cartoon of Colonel E. B. Robinson (page 11) both taken from *The Snapper* Vol XXI in the Local Studies Library, Central Library, Hull.
Dennis J. Boyle, Esq., Welwick, for permission to reproduce the photograph of Bert Hazell and Frank Robinson (page 40) of which he holds the copyright.

Published by Highgate Publications (Beverley) Ltd.
24 Wylies Road, Beverley, HU17 7AP
Telephone (0482) 866826

Printed and Typeset in 10 on 11pt Plantin by
B.A. Press, 2-4 Newbegin, Lairgate, Beverley, HU17 8EG
Telephone (0482) 882232

British Library Cataloguing in Publication Data

Cookson, David
    Robbie: the story of Frank Robinson of Patrington, East Yorkshire:
    1. Humberside. East Yorkshire (District). Agricultural industries. Farms.
    Social life, 1901- — Biographies
    I. Title
    942.8'39082

ISBN 0-948929-18-9

Cover: Patrington church (Humberside Libraries and Arts) and Frank Robinson delivering coal (daughter, Pat, in arms).

FOREWORD

by

Bert Hazell, CBE, JP, M.Univ:York

When, over 50 years ago, I was appointed by the Executive Committee of the National Union of Agricultural Workers to the post of District Organiser for the whole of Yorkshire, I was handed a list of Branch Secretaries scattered throughout the three Ridings of this vast county. Most of these were elderly, having joined the Union when it was formed in Yorkshire in 1918, but there was an exception to this general position, and that exception was Frank Robinson of Patrington.

On my first visit to the Patrington Branch, I was tremendously impressed by Frank's enthusiasm for the Union and the manner in which he was able to inspire his members. This he has maintained throughout the years.

From time to time there emerges from the ranks of farm workers someone of outstanding ability. Frank is one such person, and it became obvious to me in those early days that, given the opportunity, he would make his mark in a much wider field of public work. This has proved to be the case, as this book clearly indicates. One feature I have always admired Frank for is his remarkable memory, and, if one is discussing with him the coastline and the lost villages of the East Riding, he is able to give chapter and verse straight off the cuff; facts and figures regarding world poverty present no problem to him, whilst names and personalities within our own union or throughout the wider Trade Union and Labour Movement who were active in past years are instantly brought to mind. Just mention Local Government, and the floodgates are opened.

Frank and I spent much time together over a great many years for we had much in common. Throughout all those years he was a most able and loyal colleague and friend. This book recalls incidents which bring happy memories to me and I am sure that those privileged to read it will be inspired by Frank's enthusiastic approach to the tasks undertaken in spite of his physical handicap.

In recent years, many have paid tribute to Frank in appreciation of his services in the public sphere, both in his village and the much wider field, but I am sure the granting of the Freedom of the Borough of Holderness was his proudest hour. To lesser folk these tributes could have given a sense of superiority, but not Frank, for he is 'Robbie' to everyone in Patrington and to the many people with whom he is associated.

This book is a remarkable record of effort and achievement, and I am delighted it has been written.

The scroll presented to Frank Robinson when he was made an Honorary Freeman of Holderness Borough Council.

Chapter One

EARLY DAYS

On 10 October, 1903, in a cottage in Eastgate, Patrington, East Yorkshire, twin boys were born. Their father, Frank Robinson, was a painter and decorator; their mother, Sarah Ann, was a washer-woman, taking in washing and on some days going out to do the washing at people's houses. The boys, Frank and Tom, were strictly brought up. Their father was a real disciplinarian in table manners, conduct in the home, and cleanliness. Their mother well knew the struggle and hardship of bringing up a family, for this was her second marriage. Her first husband, William Boynton, had been a Methodist local preacher, and had walked from his home in Halsham to and from Spurn Point to take the Sunday services. Unfortunately it had poured with rain that day, and he had died of pneumonia a week later, leaving Sarah Ann a widow with three children. All five children were brought up to go to Sunday school from a very early age. Frank remembered getting up to say his recitation at the Sunday School Anniversary at only three years of age.

The twins, and their sister, Irene, went to the weekday school in Patrington at three years of age. Frank recalled being taken out of the infants' classroom to the headmistress's classroom and standing on a stool beside Miss Wilson as she sat at her desk, reciting to the top class his alphabet and the 'twice one are two' up to 'twice ten are twenty'. For this he won a penny. Frank was out of the infants' and into Standard 1 when only five, and into the senior X7 class at thirteen years old.

Surrounded by farms, the youngsters soon learned how to earn a little money — tenting pigs, tenting cows, picking stones from the fields, crow-scaring. (Tenting pigs meant going to the foldyard early in the morning with a whip and a haversack, leading 30 or 40 pigs down the street to the stubble fields, staying there in all weathers until three or four o'clock in the afternoon, and then taking the animals back to the foldyard. After the corn had been led away to be stacked there was plenty left on the ground for the pigs to pick at. Sometimes women went gleaning — picking up corn for their chickens.) All these jobs earned the boys 6d. (2½p.) per day. As they got older they were allowed to 'lead fost hoss', carry water to the steam engine on threshing days, and take lunches to the labourers at hay and

1

Frank Robinson's father, Frank.   *Frank Robinson's mother, Sarah.*

Eastgate, Patrington.
Frank Robinson was born in the cottage on the right, with the barrel outside.

harvest time. Generally, when not at school, they spent most of their time either working on the farm or riding in waggons or carts, or on horse back.

Even as a boy, Frank had the urge to travel and see the world. At the age of eleven, Tom and Frank joined the Sea Scouts. The troop at Patrington was attached to the Second Holderness Sea Scouts at Withernsea. During World War I, in their smart sailor uniforms, they did war service, helping in army canteens, running messages, and some, good at semaphore signalling and morse code, had training with the regular troops stationed in the area. At Patrington the full battalion of the 1st Leicestershire Regiment with band and drums, the Royal Engineers, Royal Army Medical Corps and Royal Army Ordnance Corps were stationed in the village from 1914 to 1919, making it like a garrison town. Frank followed them whenever he could on their fighting manoeuvres and route marches. On one occasion he received six strokes of the cane from head teacher Miss Wheatley for running away from school to be with the soldiers. He got to know the army barracks really well, for he went round the huts asking the soldiers if they wanted any washing doing. He would return home with a bag full of bundles of washing — towel, shirt, socks, pants and vest. He marked them for his mother and later, when washed and cleaned, would take them back to the camp and collect the money — 6d. or perhaps 8d. a bundle. At the age of fourteen Frank tried to join as a drummer boy. Bandmaster Witt, who played the organ at the Methodist Church, looked at him with a kindly eye, but Drummer Reffin, the silver bugler of the Leicestershire Regiment, who eventually married Frank's sister Irene, advised him no, not yet. Frank's brother George left farm work and joined the East Yorkshire Regiment. He was sent out to the front, twice wounded, and eventually taken prisoner. Patrington owed a lot to the army, for it obtained a piped water supply for the first time. The trenching for the pipes was dug by the Labour Corps, men unfit for active service.

When a pupil reached X7 at school, working in the school gardens and running errands for the head teacher, it was possible to leave school if employment was available, providing one had a good attendance and had done well in one's education. Having turned their hands to almost everything on the farm that a lad could do — making bands from plaited straw in the harvest field to tie up the sheaves; singling turnips to enable the best seedlings to grow; leading 'shim horse' as it cleaned between the rows of turnips; feeding cattle — Tom and Frank left school to work on the farm, while other boys, whose parents were able to pay for higher education, went to school in Hull. All day at harvest time they worked in the fields, then they went home while the men stayed to stook up the day's work, telling the lads not to be late in the morning. The loads of corn were led over rough and rocky roads back to the farmyard. Sometimes the ruts and wheel tracks were so deep that they sent waggons and loads completely over.

One annual custom, which no longer survives, was the Martinmas

Hirings, when the farm lads hired themselves for one year to the farmers. This took place at a time of year (11 November) when days were short and nights were long, and the roads in a terrible condition. Work on the farm was at its slackest, and Martinmas week was a festive occasion. When Hirings Day arrived, all the farm lads and lasses would gather in Patrington Market Place. Along came the farmers in horses and traps, which were stabled at the local inns. They would then barter with the farm hands as to price. The farmers looked for lads who were strong and fit, able to stand the strenuous farm life. Bargaining was keen, for a lad who was good at his job knew his worth to the farmer. Once the hiring was agreed, the farmer gave the hand a small sum of money, the 'fest', which, if accepted, bound the hand to the farmer for one year. When the twins left school, a waggoner would receive around £40 for the year, with board and lodgings. The next man would receive £30-£35, and so on down through third lad, fourth lad, *etc.*, down to 'Tommy owt', the lad leaving school at thirteen or fourteen years of age, who received only £6-£10 for the year. Tom was hired out for the year at a farm near his home for the sum of £6 with board and lodging. Frank worked at a farm a mile from his home, walking to and from work each day. He worked six days each week, from 6 a.m. to 6 p.m. for 12s. (60p.) per week. He gave it all to his mother to supplement the family income.

Frank loved life on the farm, though it had its hazards. On one occasion he was kicked in the ribs by a horse; on another he was thrown while riding and was found lying concussed in a field by some railwaymen working on the line side. Yet, in spite of this, he turned down offers of work on the railway and a job with the horse and rully man from the Withernsea Co-operative Society. By 1920, at the age of seventeen, he had learned many more skills on the farm. He could set a rig — placing upright sticks at the end of the field as aiming-points for the plough — and plough the headland (across the ends of the furrows) afterwards. He also knew how to take up a standing furrow by soiling out — filling up the furrow so it was flat for harrowing. The skills of a farm labourer were many and varied, as shown by an anecdote told by the late Arthur Jarratt:

One day, on the bus from Hull to Aldbrough, a young man looked out of the window and saw another young man singling turnips in a very big field.

'My,' he said, to no one in particular, 'a farm labourer's job must be a monotonous one!'

'What? A farm labourer's job monotonous?' said an old man nearby. 'Why, there's hoein' an' mowin' an' ploughin' an' sowin' an' 'arrowin' an' rollin' an' reapin' an' stookin' an' leadin' an' stackin' an' thackin' an' 'edgin' an' ditchin' an' dykin' an' shepherdin' an' lambin' an' milkin'...' Then he turned witheringly to the young man and said, 'An' I s'd think thou sits on a stool all day and pushes a pen!'

Another skill, not nearly so easy as it looked, was making a load of hay.

There was great pride in coming through the village with the cart piled high, roped over the top. Frank was a strong lad, and could carry 18-stone bags when threshing wheat, peas or beans. Because of this he received the full man's rate of pay, which had risen to fifty shillings per week, thanks to the Agricultural Workers' Union, which had been formed in Patrington in 1918. As a result of a harvest strike in 1920, the Union had also obtained the Saturday half day and reduced working hours. Frank started keeping pigs at home and growing potatoes on some land he had been loaned. He also became captain of the local football team. At this time he made friends with a bonny girl from Hull who came to Patrington to look after an old lady who lived opposite him. Her name was Mona Hardy, and her father was a ship's carpenter. Her Methodist family attended Argyle Street Chapel. She was standing on the doorstep one evening as Frank cycled home from work. As he approached, she called, 'Hello, Bubbles!' When Frank asked what she meant, she explained that he was always whistling 'I'm forever blowing bubbles'. Ten years later she was to become his wife, but that tune always reminded them of their first meeting. Frank still had a hankering to see the world, and applied to join the Navy, but he was turned down because of bad teeth. He then applied to join the Army, and was accepted, the recruiting officers being impressed with his excellent physique and above-average intelligence. Thus, in 1923, at the age of nineteen, he left home, much against his parents' wishes, for he had become the main bread winner as his father suffered indifferent health.

Chapter Two

ARMY TRAINING

When Frank reported to Beverley Victoria Barracks, he filled in the various papers to enable a regular weekly allowance to be paid to his mother, which she drew at the Post Office throughout his Army career. So began the life of discipline, travel, adventure, danger and excitement, years of true comradeship which took him to lands overseas. Those first weeks at Beverley were a period of strict discipline. Grouped together with some thirty more recruits from the North of England, mainly Tynesiders, Frank became a member of the 'June Squad', and for six months went through all the rigours of square-bashing, physical training, education classes, map reading, and regimental history. Confined to barracks for the first month, in order to fully learn all the correct ways of dressing and saluting, they were then allowed into the town, after duties, with their white belts, brass buttons and silver-mounted canes to walk out with, plus correct creases in their trousers. They had first to present themselves to the guardroom for inspection, and woe betide anyone who was improperly dressed or without the correct 'short back and sides' hair cut. Their smart appearance, as they swung their arms, was not only closely watched by the Commanding Officer, the late Colonel E.B. Robinson, but also by the girls of Beverley. The C.O. regularly had lads up before him for having returned to barracks and reported to the guardroom after the Last Post had been sounded, which usually resulted in days confined to barracks. Frank only stayed out late once, on his last night at Beverley Barracks. He was only outside the Barracks' wall, saying goodbye to a pretty girl, and he never appeared before the C.O. because the next morning he was on the advance party taking all the kits and baggage to the station.

The C.O., no relation to Frank, was known as 'Mad Robbie' because of his crazy antics and strict discipline. Frank was later to serve with him in the Battalion, and in later years in civilian life he sat with him on various Government committees. He always had a great liking for any ex-'Snapper', as the East Yorkshire Regiment's men were known. In later life he went blind after a severe attack of shingles, but continued to attend the National Health Executive Council for the East Riding.

Frank enjoyed the hard life at Beverley Barracks, because he was able to take part in sports, and was able to get away on a Saturday afternoon to play football for his home club, Patrington United, if they had a game in Hull. He gained his Second Class Certificate whilst at Beverley, which raised his pay by 9d. per day. He gained top marks in P.T., becoming a long distance cross-country runner and coming 2nd in the mile race at the Quebec Sports at Beverley. He was also proficient on the rifle range, gaining a 'possible' at 'grouping' (5 out of 5). Before leaving to join the 2nd Battalion at Lichfield, the men were given their first one week's leave.

On arrival at Lichfield, the depot of the North and South Staffordshire Regiments, Frank was placed in No. 7 Platoon, B Company. He remembers really going through the mill to live up to the bugle call 'B is the best of all'. Competitions between companies and platoons were keen and intense in every respect, even to the smartness and cleanliness of the barrack rooms. Frank soon learned that No. 7 Platoon had a name to be feared, and he found himself among some of the 'old sweats' who delighted in taking the mickey out of a new boy. The corporal in charge of the room was 'Bluff' Corkin, a tough, well-built man who had played rugby for Hartlepool and was also a middleweight boxer. He was a bully in many ways, and some of the more timid lads were terrified of him; the secret was to stand up to him. Bluff was determined to see how courageous his men were, and in the barracks room at night beds were cleared, a ring made and the boxing gloves

Patrington Association Football Club, 1922-23. Frank Robinson fourth from left, front row.
Back row: J. Appleby, A. Stevenson, H. Jenkins, C. Snaith, H. Calvert, F. Marsland,
C. Burnham. H. Robson. Front row: F. Fussey, G. Lawson, R. Norris, F. Robinson, S. Blenkin.

thrown at one of the men who would then be put through his paces. Frank admits he got many a pasting, but generally held his own — he was never put on the floor and the other fellow, too, always knew he'd been in a fight. Bluff chose Frank as one of his 'gang'; they were branded on the arm with a hot poker from the fire and thus became loyal members of No. 7 Platoon.

These tough measures seemed to produce results. No. 7 Platoon won pride of place in most things. Bluff was very unforgiving of failure. If a member of the platoon was detailed for guard duty, then Bluff expected him to 'win the stick', especially if he was the only one from the platoon on duty that day. Guards were generally detailed on a weekly rota, and it was up to the Company Sergeant-Major to detail men for guard duty. A 'stick man' was the man chosen by the Battalion Orderly Officer who inspected the main guard each day — he was chosen for his smartness, cleanliness and action during guard-mounting inspection. The man who won the honour did no guard duty, although it counted as one, but instead acted as messenger for the day, with belt and bayonet, stick and satchel, taking orders from the C.O.'s office when necessary, and at night able to get a good lie-in, instead of doing four hours on and eight hours off during the 24-hours, guard duty. Frank won the stick on his first main guard duty, and another three times after that. On one occasion he came very close to spoiling this good record.

Frank had been detailed for guard on the Sunday morning. On the Saturday night, instead of 'dogging' (polishing and cleaning), he went off on P.P. (permanent pass) which granted permission to be out when off duty until 12 midnight. Frank went off to Tamworth, a town three miles away, returning at midnight having spent a jolly evening with the lads down town. Getting into bed, he fell fast asleep. Next morning, as it was Sunday, he slept on, not having heard reveille, and not bothering to answer the cookhouse call. Sunday, except for Church parade and other duties, was 'beds down' all day. He was rudely awakened by his room-mates, who informed him he had half an hour to guard duty. Feeling anything but fit for main guard duty, he somehow managed to wash and shave. The lads rallied round. One lent him his rifle, already polished, another lent his tunic, and another his pack with all the brasses polished. Putting on his spare boots, always kept polished, Frank somehow tumbled down the top flight of stairs of the barrack block as the bugle was sounding 'five minutes for guard'. Fortunately for him, Bluff was away for the weekend playing rugby. The guard mounted and marched out onto the square, almost under the barrack room windows. Frank was No. 2, next to the right-hand man, Tommy Bradley, a tall ginger-haired lad from the same squad at Beverley, who was in No. 5 Platoon. He was spotlessly clean in every way, a real 'dogger bloke', always polishing and blanco-ing, boots shining like mirrors; but Tommy was as nervous as a kitten at times. After they had halted and lined up, the band and drums stopped playing and the C.O., standing out at the front facing the guard, cried out, 'Guard will fix bayonets!' Tommy shot out the necessary twelve yards, for there were two or three guards all mounting in addition to the main guard. 'Fix bayonets!' ordered the C.O., and Tommy made a hash of it. 'Get back!' shouted the C.O. 'Change places with No. 2.' So Frank became right hand man. Again the commands rang out, and this time all went well. The C.O. then carried out the usual inspection up and down the ranks and then marched back to his post. Then he marched up, stood in front of Frank and fixed him with his glare, then turned smartly round and marched back to his post. Frank felt like a robot, his head ached and he thought he could never do guard duty that day. He could hear his mates in the windows above, agog to see what would happen next. At last, 'Stick man No. 1 fall out!' came the sharp command from the C.O. Frank could hardly believe it, but the yell from the lads in the windows told him it was true, and, sloping arms, he stepped forward, gave the salute, wheeled round and took his place with the N.C.O.s as the guard did their fixing again and marched away behind the band. The C.O. then went over, looked Frank straight in the eye and said,

'And where were you last night?'

'Down Tamworth, sir.'

'Oh, and did you have a good time?'

'Rather, sir!'

'Were you drunk?'

'Hardly that, sir, but we did have a jolly time.'

'Do you like the army, lad?'

'Yes, sir, I find it challenging.'

'Well done. You'll be O.K. I was a ranker myself. Stick to it!'

And with that, Frank was dismissed. Going back to his room, he was received like a hero with No. 7.

'How did you do it, Rob? What did he say?'

'I was glad he didn't ask my rifle number,' was all Frank could reply.

Tommy Bradley never did win the stick, and eventually became an officer's batman. After Frank had won the stick three times in succession, and also having a 2nd. Class Certificate of Education, he was given a job in the cook-house.

This was a new experience, and Frank enjoyed it, even though it meant having an early call from the guard at 3-30 a.m. when he was on the rota for early morning cooks. This meant putting in his call at the guard room the night before, stating the name of the block, room number, bed position, *etc.* It was necessary to rise at this time to light all the fires and have everything boiling and ready for the others who came on duty at 7 a.m., breakfast being at 7-30 a.m.

Sergeant Moore, the Cook Sergeant, was a decent sort, and Frank got on with him all right. The large cook-house, with its big ovens, was in the centre of two dining halls seating 500 men, and from 7 a.m. to 2 p.m. all

Lance-Corporal Frank Robinson in the army (1924).

hands were busily engaged. Then from 2 p.m. the two orderly cooks remained to do their rota duty.

After a period in the cook-house, Frank was transferred to the gymnasiun as gym orderly. This involved keeping the gym clean and tidy and making tea in the morning breaks for the gym instructors and P.T. Sergeants. During his duties in this large gym, Frank was taught the skills of boxing by Teddy Telford, an army boxing champion, whom he had known at Beverley. Eventually, Frank was returned to army duties. He did well on the firing range and was soon promoted to Lance Corporal, which of course meant extra pay.

The two years at Lichfield soon passed. Twenty-five-mile route marches with band and drums and full packs were a weekly event. Summer training was at Rugeley Camp on Cannock Chase. This was followed by a spell up in Yorkshire at Catterick Camp for Brigade manoeuvres. This involved being laid out on the moors day and night for weeks in mock battle. Aircraft dropped bags of flour on those they spotted, the 'bombed' men then being deemed dead or prisoners-of-war, and being sent back to their units. Frank's company escaped and earned themselves six weeks special leave.

Opportunities to participate in sport were plentiful. Off duty afternoons were filled with football, cricket, cross-country running or rugby. Competition between companies and platoons was keen and Frank often found himself in the thick of it. In the evenings boxing matches were arranged, and often dances were held in the large gymnasium.

One of the outstanding events while at Lichfield was the presentation of new colours to the Battalion by the Duke of York, Colonel in Chief of the Regiment, who later became King George VI. On parade before reveille, the men trained hard for the occasion for weeks before the great day, under the masterly supervision of R.S.M. Percy Foster, a Hull man; even officers had to undergo his strict discipline. On the big day, thousands of spectators ringed the large parade ground of the adjoining Staffordshire Regiment and watched the grand spectacle of the marching off of the old colours and the presentation of the new. Every man gave of his best and the occasion went off to perfection and brought congratulations from far and wide. Colonel Geddes, the C.O., was so pleased that he paraded the Battalion the next day and read out all the telegrams and messages. In expressing his thanks he gave a day's holiday to everyone, even those confined to barracks.

Eventually the day arrived for which most of the men had longed — the tour of duty abroad. Frank was asked to stay behind and help to train newcomers, but he declined. He wanted to see the world and hoped to make the army his career. It was revealed that they were to be sent to Egypt. Following draft leave and a farewell dinner at a local inn organised by the corporals' mess, they were ready to depart for the Middle East. On the afternoon prior to departure, Frank had the joy of scoring the winning goal in the Company Football Shield final, bringing further honour to 'B' Company. There was time in the evening for a little celebration; next morning at 3 a.m. they were on the train for Southampton and Egypt.

Colonel E. B. Robinson, Frank's Commanding Officer: later a frequent colleague on committees.
[Humberside Libraries and Arts]

Chapter Three

LIFE OVERSEAS

In spite of it being 3 a.m. the men had a great send-off, the band and drums playing them the three miles to the station. The wives and sweethearts being left behind in England assembled at the station to say goodbye amid kisses, hugs and tears. Frank was free of such ties, having said goodbye to Sally Davis, a Birmingham lass who had been his only real girlfriend during his stay at Lichfield. He told her that he would not tie himself to any girl while he was in the army abroad, as it was not fair to either party. Another of the men corresponded with her and she always sent her love to Frank, but he lost touch and never found out whether or not she married.

As the train pulled out of Lichfield station, the band played 'The Yorkshires are a lousy lot' and 'The girl I left behind me'. They were waved away to 'Auld lang syne'. Arriving at Southampton they embarked on the troopship *City of Marseilles*, an Ellerman City Line boat, bound for Egypt. Eight hundred men left Lichfield that day.

After a pleasant voyage of twelve days, calling at Gibraltar and Malta on the way, they arrived at Port Said. They disembarked and travelled to Mustapha Barracks, Alexandria, to be billeted in wooden army huts on the shores of the Mediterranean Sea. After exchanging greetings with the lads of the 1st. Battalion, most of whom were T.X. (time expired) and were returning home, the new arrivals went to bed and were soon deep asleep, unaware that the bed-bugs were enjoying a feast on their newly-sent bodies. These large creatures had a royal time, and in the morning the men were covered from head to toe with spots and rashes. The old sweats, who, of course, had known what to expect, enjoyed the strong language which resulted. A search was made of the beds' iron legs and the 'biscuit' mattresses. Every part was washed and cleaned in paraffin oil, but the bugs persisted. Eventually, though, they became immune to the bites. Life beside the Mediterranean was grand, with plenty of bathing, and sand lizards running all around.

Frank and some of the others were posted to Mex, a large ammunition dump beside the big salt lakes. Their only duties were guard duties, and on days off they dived and swam in the warm Mediterranean. One of Frank's companions, 'Butch' Farrow, a Hull lad, received a letter from home telling him that his sixteen-year-old younger brother had been drowned at sea on his first fishing trip.

From Mex, they were sent back to 'Alex', where Frank was picked to play football against a team from the hospital, which was being played in the Palace grounds. It was King Fuad's birthday, and the game was held up at half time while the band, all in white and wearing red fezzes, marched across the pitch to take up their positions in the stand, near King Faud, who was in the royal box. Frank had a clash of heads with a Palace defender, which made several stitches necessary, but his team won 4 — 3 and his injury did not prevent him from enjoying the celebrations, entertainment and feast which they were given that night. All the streets were illuminated and decorated and many sailors joined the party, as the *Queen Elizabeth*, the flagship of the Mediterranean Fleet, was in port at the time. Frank felt a hand on his shoulder, and voice said, 'Why, it's Robbie!' He turned round to find Sid Oldfield, a lad from Patrington Haven, who was serving on the *Queen Elizabeth*. Sid eventually transferred to the Australian Navy, married a New Zealand girl, and took up residence there after he left the navy.

From Egypt, Frank's unit was transferred to North China, being relieved by the Leicestershire Regiment, whose band played them off to the station where they entrained for Suez, to embark on the old troopship *S.S. Derbyshire* to travel down the Red Sea to Aden and beyond, a voyage which took five weeks. There were 1500 troops on board, including men of the Argyll and Sutherland Highlanders, and many were the clashes with them. On one occasion, mugs and plates were thrown across the mess deck and a real battle took place. The result was a reduction in pay to cover replacement crockery and repairs. The Red Sea, which separates North East Africa from Arabia, is some 1460 miles in length and 250 miles across at its widest point, running from Suez in the north to the Straits of Bab el Mandeb and Aden in the south. It proved a sweltering voyage through one of the hottest regions in the Middle East.

Frank was in charge of half a dozen men who were responsible each day for keeping the second-class bar supplied with beer and minerals. This meant clearing away all the empties each morning and taking them down into the stores in the hold, obtaining further supplies and carrying the crates and bottles to the hatch to be hoisted up to the bar. It was an easy job and allowed plenty of time to take part in the ship's games and sports or simply lounge on deck when free. Frank loved to watch the flying-fish and dolphins jumping around the boat. They passed through Hell's Gate and the Twelve Apostles, the rocks which lie in the straits near Aden. After a short stay they sailed into the Indian Ocean, bound for Colombo, Ceylon (Sri Lanka today). During that 2,000-mile voyage they ran into a monsoon. They could see it coming towards them, with its mountainous waves, long before it reached them, and, when it struck, they were safely battened down and able to withstand the gale-force winds which at times caused the old troopship to be completely submerged. As the ship rolled and pitched, Frank was profoundly grateful not to be the lookout in the crow's nest.

On arrival at Colombo, which was used as a coaling station, they were allowed a full day ashore while the *S.S. Derbyshire* refuelled. Frank and some half dozen others hired a taxi and went off on a tour of Lipton's tea plantation. They saw the women with their baskets on their backs picking the tea leaves, and the loaded bullock carts conveying the crop to the capital city. They called at a Salvation Army canteen for minerals and refreshments, then returned to town to watch a football match, astounded to see that the natives kicked the ball with their bare feet. They also experienced their first ride in a rickshaw, which later in China was known as a shopee. Many of the soldiers got tattooed, but this did not appeal to Frank. Some of the men were almost covered from head to foot, which to Frank looked anything but beautiful. They were due back on board at 8 p.m., and there was a rush for boats to take them across to the ship anchored out in the harbour. They had to walk along planks laid across the barges lying alongside the *Derbyshire* and roared with delight when Corporal Archie Nottman missed his step and fell in. They had to haul him out with boat-hooks.

Next day they steamed away, heading for Singapore and then Hong Kong. Sports, deck games, boxing and concerts were regularly held. It was a fine sight to see the men gathered in a huge circle on deck in the moonlight, listening to Sergeant Cerrino's wife singing 'What'll I do' and 'Three o'clock in the morning'. In a six-round boxing match, Frank came up against Jimmy Holbrook. Unknown to Frank, he had won the light heavyweight championship of the Middle East Forces; as Frank was only a welterweight, fighting at catchweight, he lost on points, being bruised about the face and sporting a black eye. He and Jimmy became friends, and Frank was able to help him with his studies and teach him how to make out parade statements. Jimmy eventually became a military policeman in Tientsin.

As they approached Singapore, the climate was hot and humid, and in the Penang Straits Frank had his first real dose of sea-sickness. He had gone into the hold to see the lads in the prison cells. They looked terrible and were vomiting green. This was enough for Frank; going up on deck he did likewise and lay out on the promenade deck without any meals until he felt well enough to nibble a ship's biscuit. Having obtained a pick-me-up at the bar, he resorted to his hammock for the night. The time spent in Singapore helped him to recover, and by the time the ship left for Hong Kong he was his old self again. Some of the ship's crew, who had sailed most of their lives, told him that after a lengthy shore leave they were always sea-sick when they returned to sea.

The Scottish lads were left behind in Singapore and, accompanied by a few Royal Artillery, Royal Engineers and Ordnance Corps, they set sail on the five days' voyage to Hong Kong, lying at the mouth of the Canton River. Hong Kong is really an island, opposite Kowloon on the mainland. At that time it was one of the main military and naval stations in the Far East. As they sailed gently into Victoria Harbour they were greeted with the sirens of the naval vessels, including that of the flagship *H.M.S.Hawkins* under the command of Admiral Sinclair. Chinese junks and sampans were there in their hundreds, and with the surrounding peaks it was a splendid sight, especially at night, when the illuminations below and the stars and moon above combined to make an unforgettable scene.

Advance arrangements having been made for football and boxing competitions with the East Surrey Regiment stationed in Hong Kong, the whole battalion marched through the city, headed by the band and drums playing 'Marching through Georgia' and 'Yorkshire lass'. The regiment won both the boxing and football matches, in spite of their sea-legs.

The highlight for Frank, however, was an excursion with his old pal Tommy Johns, who had been with him since his Beverley days. They went out by naval boat to the flagship anchored in the harbour to visit his friend from civilian days, Stoker Arthur Johnson. Arthur managed to obtain shore leave and, along with twenty more naval lads, they spent many happy hours together in Hong Kong, joining with the Yorkshire soldiers. This happy interlude being over, they set sail for the cold climate of Northern China, having been warned in advance to wear fur clothes and caps in the winter months.

Frank Robinsin (with a moustache) in a rickshaw, Tientsin, China, 1926.

Chapter Four

TIENTSIN

Unable to sail up the rivers, because of the lack of deep water, the troopship steamed around the coast, past Shanghai and Weihaiwei, to the port of Chinwangtao, where the soldiers disembarked in order to travel by rail to Tientsin, which was to be the headquarters of the regiment for the next two years. The men had not been fully equipped with winter clothing, and as they felt the intense cold they had some idea of what the winter months would bring. The railway journey was slow, in carriages more like cattle-trucks, with no heating, and they were continually held up by the Chinese Civil War, which caused frequent blockages along the line. They arrived at Tientsin after thirty-two hours of discomfort. Led by the band and drums playing all the familiar marching tunes, the men marched through the town to their barracks some distance away. A fireworks display greeted their arrival (an old Chinese custom) and they turned into the barracks to the sound of the Regimental March. The barracks were occupied by the Lancashire Loyal Regiment, and the newcomers were able to swap yarns and learn something of the hazards and difficulties they would encounter. Tientsin, twenty miles up the River Pai-ho, was still a Treaty Port, split up into different concessions — American, Italian, French and English — the Chinese city being situated separately. The concessions were manned and policed by Chinese people, but the signs and names were in the language of the concession country, so the men felt quite at home. One of the largest buildings was the Gordon Hall, a reminder of the Boxer Rebellion. It was in the grounds of this hall that the parades and ceremonials took place, including a memorial service for Queen Alexandra.

The men soon settled down to life in North China. 'A' Company were sent to Peking, where they were responsible for providing the guard at the British Legation H.Q. 'D' Company were split between Weihaiwei and Fengtai, being changed at frequent intervals, which meant sea trips in old barges. 'B' and 'C' Companies remained at the Company H.Q. in Tientsin with the band and drums. The cold was so intense that after washing their hair the men found their scalps covered with ice. They had large stoves in the centre of the barrack rooms, but even so they needed plenty of rugs and blankets at night. Their clothing was more like an Eskimo outfit — fur coats, caps pulled over their ears, and goggles in case of sandstorms from the Gobi Desert. The quarters consisted of long lines of wooden huts, each with a long verandah running its length, the huts being divided into rooms just large enough for each platoon section. They had electric lights, which were still a luxury in 1925. (Withernsea did not obtain an electricity supply until 1929).

Each section leader had his room boy who 'swalled up' (cleaned the room). Frank's room boy was called Tung. He not only kept the quarters clean, but also made up the beds while the men were at breakfast, cleaned their buttons and blacked their boots. He lay on a form near the stove all night, keeping watch. If blankets or coats fell off the bed during the night, Tung would put them back. After breakfast he went home to his wife and large family, returning at tea-time around 5 p.m. Each man paid Frank 20 cents a week, which was given to Tung as his wage, a total of about 2 dollars 50 cents, plus any tips he might receive. Compared to the 15 cents a day received by most Chinese labourers, this was really good pay. If ever Tung found any money while sweeping the floor, he would take it to Frank, who would say, 'Camshaw, Tung,' which meant that he could keep it. He would graciously bow and say thankyou. Once a month he would ask if he could have the day off to go and see 'chop-chop,' the monthly public execution. These were gruesome events, but Tung went as if he were going to a gala or fair.

It was an idle life in many ways, for the Chinese boys would shave the men while they slept, for 20 cents a week. The exchange rate was fixed at 10 dollars to the pound, no matter how the rate fluctuated in the city from month to month. The officers were billeted in the best hotels in Tientsin, and the Orderly Corporal had the duty of going each night with the daily notices for them to sign. At first they travelled in the shopees, but were later provided with bicycles.

An amusing incident occurred on the first Sunday Church Parade. Being among the Nonconformist party of about fifty at the rear of the Anglicans, Frank marched into Tientsin. About a mile from H.Q. the Nonconformists wheeled off from the main parade and marched to a large Methodist Church on a street corner which had been marked on the map for them. Filing into the large church, amidst a large, silent, mainly Chinese congregation, the soldiers filled up two or three long seats in the centre. The preacher, a Chinese lady, then commenced speaking, and the steward gave out hymn sheets — all in Chinese! The organ began to play, and the congregation rose to sing — in Chinese. The soldiers then realised they were in the wrong church and had to file out quietly. Corporal Lawson, who was in charge of the party, was known as 'Chinky' Lawson from that day. They did not find the correct church but the next Sunday they did — it was a Congregational Church in the pastoral care of an Irish minister. The congregation were mostly English or American. Sometimes mid-week social events were organised, which some of the soldiers attended.

Tientsin had cinemas, open from 9 p.m. until midnight, showing films such as *The Phantom of the Opera*, (banned in England for many years), or *Charlie in the Gold Rush*, *etc.* There were also many cabarets, with guitars playing seductively to lure the men in. Mostly, white Russian girls were in attendance, and the off-duty soldiers had very enjoyable times. Sometimes trouble would break out with the American sailors, which would end with fighting and chairs being thrown. Frank still enjoyed taking part in games of football and rugby, or participating in cross-country runs of three to six miles.

Christmas Eve, 1925, was freezing cold, and Frank found himself with a Lewis gun section in an outpost called Monument Bridge. To fall asleep was almost impossible, unless one wanted to be frozen to the ground. Nearby was a small monument where a Chinese man had a stall selling monkey nuts. Frank ate more nuts then than at any other time of his life. The Chinese Civil War was still in progress, and the chances of an enjoyable Christmas seemed remote, but suddenly a message came through that there was a 48-hour cease fire and the men were allowed to return to barracks. Tung managed to obtain some 'sham-shoo-ee' (whiskey). He warmed it up in an old mug on the stove, and very soon all were sound asleep. An old rhyme says:

> 'Not drunk is he, who, on the floor,
> Can rise again and ask for more;
> But drunk is he, who prostrate lies,
> Without the power to move or rise.'

Next day, Christmas Day, they slept in, but managed to get to the mess afterwards to celebrate the festive season.

On the whole, it was an enjoyable life for the fit and hardy. There was plenty of adventure, excitement and danger. Escorting the international train to Peking, with its National flags on the front of the engine, often caused difficult problems, and on one occasion it took eleven days, the line having been blown up, and the soldiers lived on bully-beef and biscuits alongside the Great Wall which actually ended near the British fort of Shanhaikuan.

The Country Club at Tientsin was out in the country and it was there that important luncheons, *etc.*, were held. Frank was on duty on the occasion of a luncheon given by the officers in honour of a visit by H.R.H. Prince George, who was serving on *H.M.S. Hawkins*. He had come up the river by gunboat and was on his way to Peking. It was a very grand occasion, Colonel Haskard, Major Grant, Captain Jolly and all the officers being present, with C.Q.M.S. Busty Pearce at the entrance with all his medals prominent.

Many of the N.C.O.s, including Frank, were sent on a six-week Cadre

Training Course dealing with small arms and other weapons. It was with great joy that Frank learned that he and 'Tut' Temple had topped the list; promotion for the future seemed assured. In the hot summer weather the frogs could be heard croaking as the snakes hunted among them. At times they were like a flock of ducks quacking as the snakes made their bite. Cross-country running was one of Frank's favourite occupations, and he thought nothing of running three miles before reveille was blown. All was going well, but Frank received an injury to his knee which, in spite of treatment at the first aid centre, became infected. Perhaps by playing rugby on sandy pitches and with cross-country running he had helped grit to enter the wound; whatever the reason, he suffered severe pain and had to be relieved from guard duty and was taken to hospital. He remained in hospital for four months, six weeks of which were on the dangerously ill list, strapped to a Thomas's splint, a contraption like a goal-post over his bed. It was only the skill of Dr. Grice, the surgeon from the civilian hospital, which saved his life. The army doctors had the wrong ideas for treatment, having made an incorrect diagnosis. After three operations, Frank was down to six stones in weight. For three weeks he was fed on brandy and milk through a feeding tube.

As so often happens, the illness reached its crisis during the night. For once Frank had no pain; he just wanted to go to sleep, but the nurses with blocks of ice around his head were continually taking his pulse and temperature, and did their best to keep him awake. They told him afterwards that his pulse was racing at 126 and his temperature was 106°. While lying awake, Frank suddenly saw his mother standing at the foot of the bed. She looked at him, beckoned with her hand, and said, 'Come home, come home, son.' Then she disappeared as suddenly as she had come. Frank realised that he was dying; that if he went to sleep it would be the end. Longing to see his mother's face again, he fought against the drowsy sleepy feeling. After more swabbing with icy water, more pulses and temperatures being taken, at last he was greeted by smiles from the M.O. and the

Frank Robinson on crutches, recuperating in hospital, China (1927).

nurses. They told him the crisis was past and he could go to sleep. After an injection of morphia he did just that. It was not until the following year, after returning home, that Frank heard an interesting story. His mother had received a cablegram from China, informing her that her son was lying dangerously ill. She and her brother, a police sergeant in Hull, got down together on their knees and prayed. On looking at the cablegram, Frank saw that it was received around 4 p.m., approximately midnight in Tientsin on the very day when he saw the vision of his mother at the foot of his bed. Frank said later, 'Was my life saved in answer to a mother's prayer? God alone knows.'

Frank's recovery was very slow, and often he did not receive any mail from home for many weeks, due to the Civil War. The warring factions threatened the British and foreign interests which had been secured by treaty before the First World War. This was the reason for the garrisoning of strategic points along the Peking-Tientsin Railway, which delayed the mail. Most of the mail came by the Siberian Railway, which normally took fourteen days, so that news to and from home took some time. In addition to this, Frank was unable to write for several weeks, but one of the nurses wrote to his sister to inform her of his condition. After many long weeks, Frank was able to get around on crutches. Then he obtained permission to go out in the rickshaws and so was able to visit his pals back in the barracks and make a few trips to the shopping centre of Tientsin. The 'shopee-wallahs' were always polite and treated him kindly, so he always tipped them generously. These rickshaw men usually slept under their shopees, and it was not unusual to find one lying dead in the morning.

At the Quebec Sports in Tientsin, Frank had a seat in the best stand and watched Corporal Shufflebottom, a Hull man, beat the 1924 Olympic

Sports, Tientsin — Ernie Shufflebottom beats Eric Liddell. October, 1926.

champion Eric Liddell in the 200 metres. Liddell, later to become famous as the subject of the film *Chariots of Fire*, was out in China as a missionary. He had refused to run in the 100 metres in the Olympics because the heats fell on a Sunday, which conflicted with his religious beliefs. Instead, he took the gold medal in the gruelling 400 metres after leading all the way. Liddell was known to Frank, who had played against him at rugby while in China. He was taken prisoner by the Japanese in World War II and died in a prison camp.

Chapter Five

THE LONG RETURN HOME

When considered fit to travel, Frank was transferred to the hospital at Hong Kong, being carried on a 1,500-ton China Navigation boat, the *Kui-chow*. Before he left Tientsin he was visited by two boxers, Jimmy Holbrook and Freddie Appleton. Frank admits that as the ship's bell clanged there was a tearful parting. The passage on the *Kui-chow* was far from smooth. It took two days to get out of the river, being held up at the mouth until they could get sufficient depth of water to cross the bar. When at last they managed it, the propellers churned and throbbed as they crossed into the Yellow Sea. Travelling at only 20 knots, they ran into rough weather, Frank again suffering sea-sickness and confined to his cabin. The Chief Engineer was a Liverpool man, and Frank was able to hobble across to his cabin, where they became good friends. It took twelve days to get to Hong Kong, calling at Shanghai and Canton. Frank enjoyed watching the huge whales sending up their great fountains of water.

There were many Chinese on board, who slept aft, and some were smuggling coins and silken goods, hiding them in packets in the fern tubs which decorated the passenger quarters. Frank stayed in his cabin instead of going for dinner, which was set out for the passengers in the dining-room. On one occasion he discovered the Chinese boys hiding their packets in the tubs, the result being that the smugglers were put off the ship at Shanghai, the Customs officers being called in. It was a profitable game, because of the exchange rates.

On arrival at Hong Kong Frank noticed the flagship in the harbour. He was put into a coffin-like box to be carried 3,000 feet up the mountain to the hospital overlooking the harbour. Every night at 9 p.m. the guns were fired from the battery at Kowloon. The hospital sister was stern and strict, but kind, and Frank was able to get a message across to the flagship to inform his pal, Arthur Johnson, that he was in the hospital. Next day, sitting out on the hospital verandah, he watched Arthur in his naval uniform walking up the winding pathway to the hospital and was able to give him a wave long before he reached him. They had a lot to talk over, because the *Hawkins* had been in action on the Yangtze and down the 600 miles to Hankow. They obtained the sister's consent for Frank to visit the flagship, and next day the pilot boat picked him up on the quay. He was helped aboard up the ladder and was honoured to be met at the top by Prince George, later the Duke of Kent, who chatted to him and asked about the regiment. Frank was grieved in later years to hear of the Duke's death in an air crash.

After some weeks in Hong Kong, Frank was marked fit for travel and put in the hospital quarters aft of the troopship *S.S. Nuralia*. The trip lasted 56 days, calling at Singapore, Bombay and Karachi, where they stayed for ten days while troops bound for Rawalpindi went to their new station and others returned. The men were allowed ashore each day and they went sight-seeing. This included a ride in a camel-drawn rully down to the river, where they witnessed hundreds of crocodiles idly lying in the water, while native boys hopped from back to back across to the other side. Lovely black and white squirrels ran around, and swarms of locusts descended upon them.

Leaving Karachi, they called at Bombay, where Frank managed to get ashore around sunset. He saw the whole crowd salaaming and bowing in worship. Frank made friends with the ship's cook, Jack Hare, an ex-professional boxing champion. The M.O. from Tientsin, Major Hingstone, also returned home on that ship. From Bombay they crossed to Aden, and then to Port Sudan on the Red Sea, where they stayed for a week to disembark the Border Regiment who were bound for Khartoum, and awaited others who were returning home. The stay was full of interest, the harbour seemingly full of dolphins, porpoises, swordfish and sharks. Being aft, near the shute from Jack Hare's galley, Frank watched the little fish pulling at the food waste, then scattering as the big fish came along. The climate was humid and hot, and, as he lounged on the deck listening to the band, Frank heard the tune 'Valencia' for the first time. Homeward bound, they sailed up the Suez Canal into the Mediterranean Sea, calling at Malta and Gibraltar, eventually arriving at the Needles in the English Channel. They had to wait until morning before they were able to sail up the Solent into Southampton. As Frank left the ship, Jack Hare gave him a book about his life as a boxer. He was sorry to leave the ship and would have gladly travelled round the globe with her.

The hospital train pulled in beside the troopship, and the surgical cases were transported to Netley Hospital. They were housed on the top floor, giving marvellous views of the Solent and all the big liners such as the *Majestic* and *Mauretania*, as they sailed in and out on their regular voyages to America. It was a fine hospital, tremendous in size, and the Matron was a veteran of the South African War with a chest full of medal ribbons on her smart uniform. Frank was able to hop around the wards on his crutch, taking details of the new arrivals. The colour of the tabs at the foot of the bed indicated from which part of the world the patient had come — red for the Far East, blue for the Middle East, yellow for the West Indies and white for the home station. This enabled cases who had been in plague areas to be isolated. One man, a corporal, had been bitten by a camel in the Middle East, causing severe poisoning. He had to undergo many operations and was bedfast. In spite of this he ran a book on the horse racing and even the nurses used to have a 'flutter'.

Frank spent a happy Christmas at Netley, and after several weeks the time came for him to depart. On the last night he lay awake into the early hours, wondering what the future might hold. He heard approaching footsteps and pretended to be asleep. He heard Sister Cullen, an Irish girl, say, 'Such a nice lad; we're sorry he's going.' Then she bent down and kissed him on the forehead. He never forgot that kiss in the night. Next morning, with an escort from the R.A.M.C., he set off for home. The escort lived at Nottingham, so Frank said he could find his own way home from Sheffield. Then he signed the paper to certify that he had arrived home safely, dating it two days ahead so that the escort could go home and see his family. Arriving at Hull Paragon Station, Frank was pleased to see the Patrington train on the next platform. Helped by a porter who carried his kitbag, Frank was soon on the last stage of his journey home. The village postman, Mr. Gibson, was on the train and carried the kitbag home from Patrington station. The homecoming was a joyful one, though tinged with sadness, and Frank's parents were overjoyed to see him so cheerful in spite of his permanent disability.

The convalescence was long; the strain of the journey took its toll, and for several weeks Frank was seriously ill. It was some months before he was able to get about again and meet his old friends. He attended hospital frequently and after two years was officially discharged with a permanent pension. The girl who had called him 'Bubbles' was employed by his cousin at a shop in Hull. They had corresponded regularly throughout his army service, and on 18 April they were married at Argyle Street Chapel in Hull.

Frank and Mona Robinson on their wedding day.

Chapter Six

CIVVY STREET

Although pleased to be home among family and friends again, Frank regretted the loss of a promising career in the army. On the other hand, he was lucky to be alive and thanked God for His saving grace. Life was difficult in 'Civvy Street'. There was mass unemployment, and there were long queues of men outside the Unemployment Office in Patrington Market Place, which paid out benefits for Withernsea also. Frank was determined not to join that army if at all possible, and he accepted casual work on the farms. Eventually he found regular employment with a local coal dealer and general carter, a grand old man, Mr. G.M. George, an ex-Marine, who also had a small agricultural holding. Frank worked for him for five years, eventually being offered the business in 1935 when Mr. George retired. He purchased the business from his limited savings, rather than risk unemployment.

While helping the local farmers one year with the hay harvest, Frank fell off a load of hay and was seriously injured. In spite of this, he managed to struggle along somehow. Farmworkers had no unemployment scheme to fall back on in the early 1930s, and it was not until 1936, following strong pressure from the National Union of Agricultural Workers (N.U.A.W.), that the government finally allowed them within the Unemployment Insurance Act.

Frank and Mona, his wife, lived next door to a life-long trade unionist, Zach Bemrose, one of the pioneers of the 1918 era, when the Patrington branch of the N.U.A.W. was formed. Frank had rejoined the Union on his return, and was appointed branch secretary in place of George Stephenson, who was a sick man. He found that the books and paperwork had been neglected, and interest was flagging, no doubt due to the large numbers out of work in those difficult years between the two wars. The branch was still functioning due to the loyalty of a few old stalwarts, but there were fewer than twenty members. Wages were only 35 shillings a week; Frank was selling coal at 1/9d. and 2/- for a hundredweight bag, but many could not even afford that and many customers soon got into debt. There was, of course, no Social Security, Supplementary Benefit or Family Allowances.

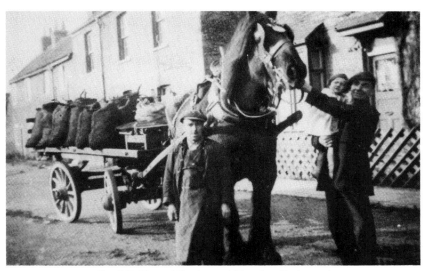

Frank Robinson delivering coal (Daughter Pat in arms).

Many farmers were going bankrupt and much good farm land lay uncultivated and derelict. Frank called special meetings of the Union at Patrington and Sunk Island and began to encourage recruitment. His army experience was a great help to him, especially in addressing meetings. The strength of the branch began to increase, and Frank received help and advice from the Yorkshire organisers of the day, Billy Crawford from Doncaster and Harry Moulson from Bilton, who was also on the Union's National Executive. Zach Bemrose was also a tower of strength. During that year a hundred members enrolled, and in three years the branch had over 300 members on its register. From this small beginning, Frank's trade union activities were to take him all over the country and abroad to Europe. In 1936 he was awarded the T.U.C. Diploma for special organising service; it was presented by Sir Walter Citrine, the General Secretary of the T.U.C.

Patrington branch had become a force to be reckoned with, holding annual dinners followed by speeches from prominent Members of Parliament — Tom Williams (later Minister of Agriculture), Tom Smith, Dave Quibell — and from officials of the N.U.A.W. — President Edwin Gooch and General Secretary Billy Holmes. The Branch Chairman, Zach Bemrose, was nominated for the National Executive Committee, and succeeded in winning a seat, previously held by Harry Maulson who had served on the N.E.C. for ten years and then taken over as District Organiser for Yorkshire following Billy Crawford's retirement. Unfortunately, Harry Maulson had to retire after six months due to ill health. It was then that Bert

27

Hazell took over as the Organiser for the whole of Yorkshire. He was a keen young live-wire from Norfolk, and a fine orator. He addressed his first meeting in Patrington in 1937, when the membership for Yorkshire was a mere 700.

Meanwhile, Frank had his coal business to look after, and he found it necessary to employ a regular man to assist him. He had added to his family over the years; Gerald had been born in 1932, and Patricia in 1938. Pat was born at the new house near the stables and coal sheds, right in the centre of the village. At weekends and sometimes during the week, Frank addressed union meetings all over Yorkshire. He was elected onto the Yorkshire County Committee, and went campaigning and addressing open-air meetings with District Organiser Bert Hazell. One Saturday night, when he was standing on a soap-box in Pocklington Market Place, some hecklers appeared among the crowd that had gathered, but they seemed to help his flow of words, rather than hinder him. When he stepped down to let others have a go, General Secretary Billy Holmes, wearing his familiar large trilby hat, thumped Frank on the back and said, 'Hey lad, we're looking for lads like thee — why doesn't thou become an Organiser?'

To his surprise, Frank replied, 'Why, I did apply, but you turned me down and never asked to see me.'

'Oh,' he said, 'when?'

'Three years ago,' replied Frank, 'but it's too late now. I've a small business and a wife and two children to keep.'

Frank kept up the good work, however, and succeeded in being elected to the Union's biennial-conference in London and made a promising debut at his first large conference.

By this time, war clouds were gathering in Europe with the rise of Adolf Hitler and the Nazi regime. Once again agriculture was recognised as a vital industry. The Government became concerned and began to press for greater food production. Land which for years had lain idle, or been sown down to grass, came under cultivation again. However, in September 1939, when war became a reality, with its blackouts and air raids, many lads were called up to the forces. In Patrington a company of the East Yorkshire Territorials was formed in May, 1939, consisting mostly of lads of 18 years of age. They were all called up into the regular forces on the day war was declared. Owing to his injury, Frank was unfit to join the army, but he did enrol as a Special Constable. He worked at his coal trade by day and did police duty at night and at the weekends. Bureaucracy, however, was not aware of Frank's past record, and one day he received his call-up papers with orders to report to the recruiting office in Hull. Not telling them of his previous army service, Frank reported as directed. Along with some 30 others, he was marched across Hull to Burton House. Having listened to a Cockney sergeant from the Education Corps who told them what the army was all about, they were then given some written examinations. They were then marched back to Jameson Street for medical examinations. Having undergone all the stages of scrutiny since 10 a.m. and then having been kept waiting for the medical until 3 p.m., Frank asked if he could have his medical so that he could get back to his business. 'You keep quiet and wait your turn,' he was told. Frank then showed the sergeant his red discharge book and asked him to show it to the M.O. The sergeant changed his attitude immediately and within a short time Frank was ushered into the large medical room in which many men in their 'birthday suits' were undergoing various examinations. He was called to a table occupied by a portly major who was reading Frank's army records. The major apologised for having kept him waiting for so long. 'No need to undress completely; let's just see your leg,' he said. The M.O. then asked him about China, whom he had served with, and did he know Major Hingston of the R.A.M.C.? 'Well I ought to, Sir,' he replied. 'He was the M.O. at Tientsin Military Hospital and he travelled home with me on the same troopship.' They chatted for a while, then the Major informed Frank that he had topped the examinations in the morning. 'I cannot order you into the army,' he said, 'but, if you care to volunteer, I may accept you as an instructor at some depot.' Frank told him that he had a business which would have to be disposed of — could he be compensated? The reply was in the negative, so Frank returned home to family and business.

Zachariah Bemrose (Chairman, N.U.A.W., Patrington branch) (left).
Frank Robinson (Secretary, N.U.A.W., Patrington branch) (right). 1931.

Chapter Seven

HECTIC YEARS

On 2 January, 1942, Frank's wife Mona presented him with twin boys, bringing the number of offspring up to four. Frank's mother, who had been bedfast for some years, was overjoyed at the news, because she had been 38 when Frank and Tom were born, and both Frank and Mona were 38 when the twins arrived. When Frank told his mother that they intended to call the boys David and Trevor, being somewhat deaf she replied, 'David's a grand name, but Clever — he'll be clever enough without calling him that!' Her forecast in some ways turned out correct, for David became a nursing officer, and Trevor, after nine years in the Parachute Regiment, in which he attained the rank of Staff Sergeant, became Assistant Manager of the North East region of Securicor.

About the time the twins were born, Frank received a letter from the General Secretary of the N.U.A.W. asking him to consider accepting a post as District Organiser for North Yorkshire, the membership having increased to such an extent that two District Organisers were needed for Yorkshire. After considering his family and business ties, Frank declined the offer, but instead stood as a candidate for the National Executive Committee and was elected to represent the Northern Counties, which included at that time Yorkshire, Lancashire, Cheshire, Northumberland, Durham, Westmorland and Cumberland. This committed Frank to a great deal of time attending monthly meetings in London, campaigning in the counties and addressing weekend conferences. Jack Brocklebank from Catwick, who had been doing good work around the Leven area, became District Organiser for North Yorkshire. During August of that year Jack, Frank and Bert Hazell set off together campaigning and organising branches throughout the whole of the North Riding. Jack had no lodgings at that time and they went from village to village, staying anywhere they could on the bed and breakfast principle. Later Jack found a house at Dishforth known as Rose Cottage.

In this way started Frank's 28 years service on the N.E.C. When he retired in 1970 due to ill health, he was the senior long-serving member. In the wartime years with their great food production drive, membership of the N.U.A.W. had increased tremendously. When Frank first joined the N.E.C. in London he found that, including General Secretary William Holmes and President Edwin Gooch, eight of the thirteen members were from Norfolk. This was because the Union had mainly been an East Anglian movement from its foundation in 1906 until its expansion in 1918. Hubert Luckett from Kent was another newly-elected member, he and Frank serving together over 25 years.

Tom Williams was Minister of Agriculture during the war, and Lord Woolton became Minister of Food. Frank often served on delegations from the N.E.C. to meet them and discuss food rationing and special concessions for farm-workers, which resulted in many supplementary rations and meat pie schemes being introduced in rural areas. Further delegations to the Minister of the Board of Trade secured special clothing coupons, wellington boots and thermos flasks, for which land drainage and forestry workers and roadmen all became eligible. Many branches of the Women's Land Army, a fine agricultural labour force, also joined the Union and received certain concessions. Frank also served on the War Agricultural Executive Committee (W.A.E.C.) in the East Riding. Thanks to this body, farmworkers could produce their employment cards in order to receive reconditioned service battle dress, dyed green, from clothing retailers who had been given supplies.

All these benefits proved valuable, and much time was taken up in meetings to discuss such matters. After one long meeting in a packed room at Guisborough, North Yorkshire, an old lady with long skirts and a large umbrella rose to address the meeting at question time. She wished to know how she could obtain some wellington boots. She became quite cross on being told she had to produce an employment card, but was given some good advice nevertheless.

The war years were very hectic for Frank, for, in addition to his London visits, his campaigning, his work on the W.A.E.C. and his coal business and small holding, he also served on the Hull and District Employment Committee, the Court of Referees and Military Tribunals. He also continued his duties as Special Constable, often being on duty all night during the intensive bombing raids on Hull and the East Coast, the German planes passing over Patrington on their way to Hull. Often as they passed over the coastline, their bombs fell on the land and villages of Holderness, causing damage and destruction to many members' homes and property. On one such raid a land-mine dropped in a field, killing seven beasts and burying one of Frank's horses. He found it covered in mud, but it had to be destroyed because of shrapnel in its knee. Incendiary bombs, Very lights and shrapnel from the guns at Kilnsea and Spurn Point firing at German planes sometimes fell in the Patrington area. The 'butterfly' anti-personnel bombs fell all over the place one weekend and the police and Specials were out in full force, walking over the fields seeking out and marking the bombs with sticks, ready for the Royal Engineers to dispose of them. A few fatalities were caused by these bombs, which resembled a large three-leaf plant when open on the ground.

One day the chattering of machine-gun fire and the rush of an aircraft hurtling towards the earth told the villagers that their gunners had hit the target, which smashed into the ground near a lonely cottage in Winestead Woods. At the crack of dawn two members of the N.U.A.W., Nellie and Doris Sutton, who lived in the cottage with their father and a third sister, Alice, went out to the scene of the crash. It was a gruesome sight; bits of bodies were strewn around, and the plane was still burning, with the headless body of a German roasting among the wreckage. Returning to their cottage, they saw what looked like a large white sheet hanging on a hawthorn bush. On the ground beside it was a German airman. Going forward cautiously, Nellie took his revolver from him and shouted for her father, but he had left home for work. Observing that the German had injured his foot when landing after baling out, they conveyed him to the cottage on an improvised stretcher. Doris then walked three miles to the nearest telephone and called the police. While they were waiting they gave the German hot drinks and food.

This was only one of several incidents involving German planes shot down in the area. One early morning another came down in two pieces, one each side of the railway line. Frank's oldest boy, being then twelve years old, went out to look at their horse and brought back several parts of the wreckage. Another young German, a fine blond-haired lad who only looked about seventeen years old, baled out wounded and fell in Ings Lane, Patrington. He was carried on a sheep-gate to a large house in Westgate which was being used as a military hospital. He was so grateful to the medical staff for their kindness that he gave one his watch. He died some days later.

During Frank's visits to London there were many alarms and near misses. On one occasion, while he was travelling to London during the night, the train was machine-gunned by enemy planes and they pulled into a tunnel near Peterborough and waited in solid blackness for an hour and a half. The Union's head office staff moved out to Bushey, near Watford, and the N.E.C. meetings were held there. For other sub-committees and deputations to Government departments, however, it was necessary to stay in London. Usually Frank shared digs with Hubert Luckett, his friend from Kent N.U.A.W.

One night they had obtained rooms on the third floor of a block of flats off the Gray's Inn Road when a severe air raid took place. The exploding bombs shook the building. Looking out, they saw the sky lit by the flames of a large building on fire. Thinking it might be the Union's head office, Frank said, 'Come on, Hubert, it's our headquarters ablaze!' Frank, having some idea that a raid could take place, had not undressed, but lay under the top blanket with his jacket and shoes off. Hubert, however, clad only in his pyjamas, slipped on his coat and slippers. The landlady, Mrs. Platts, told them to take the key as her husband was on duty with the Fire Service, and she would be in bed when the all-clear sounded. The huge blaze was the Mount Pleasant Post Office, the largest sorting office in the country. The street was cordoned off to keep out the people who were watching the firemen fight the blaze, but a police sergeant was calling for volunteers to help with the rescue work. Without hesitation, Frank was under the ropes and into the burning building, helping to get out some of the injured and handling what seemed like thousands of mail-bags. The helpers formed a chain, Frank having a Scotsman on one side of him and a Norwegian on the other. They worked like slaves until 3 a.m. when they got the order to stand clear, as the burning timbers made it unsafe to remain any longer. They were told that hot tea and cakes were on the way, and asked to give their names and addresses, but, having come from a furnace temperature, they now felt cold and decided not to wait, but return to their lodgings. They shook hands and made off. During all this time, Frank had not given a thought to Hubert Luckett and it was not until he met a hatless figure dressed only in coat and pyjamas that he realised it was Hubert. 'Good heavens, man, what are you doing?' asked Frank. 'You've got the key of the lodge,' he said, 'and I thought you were dead.' In spite of this they remained friends for another 22 years and were known as the E.C. twins.

Farm Sunday, Beverley (1940). Frank Robinson with trilby hat and walking-stick.

33

Chapter Eight

VISITS AND CAMPAIGNS

During all this activity, campaigning in Yorkshire continued, and up in the North Riding with Jack Brocklebank, the District Organiser, they enrolled a hundred members in one week. One day, near Ripon, they found a herd of cattle blocking the road. In spite of all Jack's efforts with the car horn, the herd merely gazed at them with mild curiosity. Frank got out to clear a way, but no sooner had Jack got through than the cattle decided to chase him. Up went their tails, and Jack had to drive in top gear for a mile before he was clear. Frank was left behind with the beastman, who expressed his opinion quite forcibly. Frank took the opportunity to ask him to join the Union. One meeting followed a parish council meeting, and Frank had to face a barrage of questions from farmers, grocers, a farrier and a schoolmaster. He gave a good account of himself and was cheered at the end.

Up in Northumberland, where the District Organiser was Jack Davidson, Frank addressed a crowded meeting in a public bar. An army sergeant shouted, 'Why don't you join the army?' 'Before you came up, chum,' replied Frank, 'with a good leg and a swinger as a souvenir.' The sergeant apologised afterwards and bought Frank a drink.

The problems for Union Organisers in the later stages of the war were many and varied. German and Italian prisoners-of-war were working on the land, and there was a case of a farmer using P.O.W.s to evict a farmworker from his cottage. The Union took this up with Mr. Hudson, who was Minister of Agriculture at that time, and he ordered that P.O.W.s should be used for farm work only. Exploitation of child labour was rife in those days, and another deputation to the Ministry obtained an undertaking that children under 14 years of age should not be employed for more than four hours per day. Wages were fixed on a national basis under the Defence of the Realm Act (D.O.R.A), which transferred all authority from the County Wages Boards to the National Wages Board in London. The East Riding, on 60 shillings a week, was five shillings better off than many counties. The National Wages Board brought all counties into line with this, and, in spite of deputations, the East Riding lost its five shilling advantage, although, of course, many counties gained five shillings. Mechanisation was developing fast, with tractors replacing the familiar horses. This greatly helped the productivity drive and made possible the ploughing of more acres to help defeat Hitler's blockade of food supplies.

By 1943, the fourth year of the war, people fully realised the importance of agriculture to the war effort. Many men and women from all walks of life had come to work on the land, and membership of the Union continued to increase rapidly. Kent became known as 'bomb alley' as V1 and V2 flying bombs passed overhead regularly. Those were dark days, there seeming to be no end to the war in sight. Coming up from the underground station at King's Cross one night, where thousands of families took their night's lodgings during the blitz and where many a child was born, Frank saw a large poster showing Christ holding a lantern and the words 'I am the Light of the world'. It was things like this that gave renewed hope and the inspiration to carry on.

1943 saw the Silver Jubilee of the Patrington branch of the N.U.A.W., which by then had 350 members. They determined that never again would agriculture be treated as it had been in those bleak years between the wars but would be given the recognition it deserved as a major industry.

As the Executive member for the Northern Counties, Frank was detailed to help Jack Davidson, the Northumberland D.O. Jack loved the Cheviot Hills which extend along the borders of England and Scotland. In places they reach over 2,500 feet, and the only uses to which they can be put are sheep farming and forestry. Up in the far North, Jack Davidson had established two branches of forestry workers, so, along with Jack Lambley, the National Organising Secretary, they decided to visit these outposts. As the D.O.'s car wheezed up the hills and careered down crazy roads, they saw sheep here and there and occasional stone buildings which were shepherds' cottages. The weather was atrocious, with blizzards of snow and hail and biting cold winds. Jack Davidson somehow kept the old car going while Frank and Jack Lambley sat in the back 'like two frozen ducks'. They talked about the intrepid explorers who had perished in the Arctic and Antarctic wastes and Frank recalled his days in North China. Just as they were beginning to wonder if they still had any hands and feet, they saw some signs of life — a camp consisting of a few buildings. They had arrived at Kielder. As the steaming and panting car drew up in front of a large log cabin, Frank had the impression that they had somehow arrived in Canada. Rushing out to meet them were some two dozen men dressed in rubber boots, thick lumber jackets and trousers, and fur lug-caps. They were very pleased to receive their visit. The men were tough and hardy, many of them ex-miners who had accepted work in the forests rather than be on the dole. Inside the log cabin, beside a welcome roaring fire, beating their feet in a tattoo to restore circulation, they learned of the working conditions of these men. The nearest town was 35 miles away; it was nine miles to the nearest public house and, should that run out of beer, it was a further nine miles to the next. Anything sent from the town had a carriage fee to be paid; even a small box of pills cost 7d. The men all paid one shilling per week into a doctor's club box, because the doctor's fee for a visit was 25 shillings. The camp shop was open twice a week, unless the weather was bad, when it was often closed for weeks on end. A small school had been built to give the dozen or so little children the rudiments of education. The men received about 4/6d. above the usual agricultural rate, but they had 4 shillings deducted for a cottage and the usual deductions for insurance and tax. Having enjoyed a well-prepared meal and hot drinks, the Union delegation promised to work towards improving their conditions, then they departed for Kershopefoot on the Scottish borders. Here too they found poor conditions. The parents had to pay £5 per year to send their children to school six miles away. Carriage on a loaf of bread was 9d. and it cost two shillings for a bottle of milk to be transported by rail.

The following summer, Frank was invited to visit the estate of Sir Arthur Munro Sutherland, who owned over 10,000 acres in the Cheviots. The estate contained about ten shepherds' cottages, well built and possessing modern conveniences such as bathroom, hot and cold water, sanitation and electric light operated from the estate's own generator. Some of these cottages were miles apart, hidden from view by the twists and curves of the burns and crags. They gave magnificent views over the valleys and across the hills. Here and there were waterfalls, and crags of solid rock where falcons built their nests. The crystal clear streams stocked with trout and salmon, the heather, or 'ling' as the local people call it, the shepherds with their dogs and sheep scattered everywhere — all these combined to make a picture of unforgettable beauty.

There were 8,000 sheep on Sir Arthur's estate, each shepherd being responsible for up to 1,000. Twice each day he drove them from the valley to the top of the hill, and the sheep gradually grazed their way down again. Frank watched one shepherd at work. The dogs rounded up the sheep which climbed the hill in single file over stone and rock, seeming to know exactly what was expected of them. The shepherds wore boots with upturned toes, specially made for climbing. They knew their job, their fathers and grandfathers having done it for generations before them. Each man had his own cow or goat and a small patch of garden. The tradesman's van visited them once a week, and the coalman once a year, bringing perhaps three tons of fuel. The sheep were the blackfaced variety, other breeds being unable to survive the high altitudes. Here Frank found what must have been one of the smallest schools in England — one room with eleven scholars whose age ranged from 5 to 13 years. The teacher, Mrs. North, was a Northumbrian by birth but had taught in Dewsbury and Coventry. One pupil had just won a scholarship to the Duke's School at Alnwick, which showed what a high standard of education was achieved. Sir Arthur, a well known shipping magnate, was a model landlord. He made his workpeople comfortable and happy and paid them well. In return they gave him faithful and efficient service. Frank thought of the contrast between this solitary, peaceful life and the bustle and danger of wartime London. As Frank returned, he found himself humming the popular song of the day, 'Shepherd of the hills I hear you calling'.

In November, 1944, Frank was again in Northumberland, staying at Mr. Gibson's farm at Nesbit where Jack Raines was the foreman. German prisoners were picking potatoes while Land Army girls took them away with a horse and cart. While there, Frank received news from his brother Tom that their mother had died. She had attained the age of 78, and had been bedfast for six years, but had never lost her faith in the life beyond. Frank returned at once, in spite of the heavy programme planned for that weekend, and saw his mother laid to rest. His father, failing in health, was looked after by old Annie, his housekeeper. She had cared for old Mrs. Robinson for twelve years, and agreed to stay on to look after Mr. Robinson, with the assurance of the home and chattels when he passed on.

1944 also saw the retirement of Billy Holmes as General Secretary of the Union under the new rules laid down at the biennial conference, which set an age limit of 65. Billy had been a great fighter for the farmworkers' cause for over forty years. He was a past Chairman of the T.U.C. and it was agreed that some recognition should be made of his valuable service. Frank was again elected to the Executive Committee. During 1944, too, another District Organiser was appointed to cover West Yorkshire.

1945 began with the new General Secretary, Alfred Dann, taking office, having been elected by 62% of the votes of the members throughout the country. He had served the Union as head of the Legal Department after returning from service in the armed forces during World War I. Using his legal background acquired before 1915, and his knowledge of farmwork, his work had been outstanding. Becoming leader of the Agricultural Central Wages Board, his ambition was to secure for agriculture and the farm workers a place in the post-war world which would always give recognition of the industry's place as essential to Britain's future prosperity. The membership of the Union was still increasing as campaigns were held throughout the country.

Once, when returning from a meeting in North Yorkshire, Frank and Jack Brocklebank ran into foul weather, with rain and thunder. They motored into two feet of water which had flooded the road for about a hundred yards. Not being an amphibious vehicle, the car 'conked out'. Like a true Yorkshireman, Jack divested himself of his shoes and socks, rolled up his trousers and, gasping as his feet entered the icy water, gallantly made his way to a nearby village and knocked on the door of the first house showing a light. The occupier happened to be the village policeman and, having convinced himself that the bedraggled and shivering figure before him was not an escaped P.O.W., he invited Jack in and furnished the hospitality for which Yorkshire folk are famous. Later, equipped with thigh boots, the two of them salvaged the car from the floods.

On another occasion, Jack was rehearsing one of his fine speeches at the boarding house where he and Frank were staying. As he emphasised a point with the great vigour and enthusiasm for which he was noted, a wave of his arm sent crashing a highly coloured ornamental vase on which the landlady placed great sentimental value. Jack replaced the vase with one even more colourful and was forgiven, but he was careful after that not to rehearse so vigorously.

By this stage in the war, victory was in sight. Frank addressed a meeting of the Women's Land Army at Darlington, all of them looking smart in their uniforms of green jersey, breeches and long socks. He paid high tribute to the contribution made by the girls to the war effort. It was at this time that graded scales for farm workers were first discussed, which would give special rates of pay for skilled workers, as in other industries. Meetings were held up and down the country to explain the advantages and disadvantages, and how the lines of demarcation would be decided. Many heated arguments ensued. At one packed meeting at Chathill, Northumberland, which went on into the late hours of the night, a young lad got up and said, 'Mister, I think the most important man on the farm is the loose-man.'

'Hear, hear!' was the general chant. In Yorkshire the loose-man is called 'Tommy Owt', meaning the man who can turn his hand to anything. It was to be 25 years later, after many arguments for and against, that such a wages structure was introduced for agricultural workers.

Chapter Nine

VICTORIES

By mid-summer, victory in Europe had been gained by the Allies, but the war in the Far East against Japan remained to be won. The coalition government, which had served the nation well under Winston Churchill since 1940, was under discussion by all parties. Churchill said that the coalition should remain until full victory was won or else there should be an immediate general election. Labour M.P. Miss Ellen Wilkinson put the case admirably when she said that an election should be held when conditions would give a fair opportunity to all the electors, not least the servicemen and women, in order that they could learn the problems and get to know the candidates. There had been no election since 1935. Churchill, however, refused the request for an autumn election and described the longevity of the present parliament as 'a serious constitutional lapse'. The Conservatives preferred a rush election on an admittedly imperfect electoral register. One newspaper reported at the time, 'In throwing down the ultimatum, the Tory Party has stood on the wrong end of a rake which may come up and smack them in the eye.'

When the snap election took place, Bert Hazell, a District Organiser for the N.U.A.W., was selected as candidate for Barkston Ash, being one of six Union members who fought the election, three successfully. Frank campaigned in support of Bert, helped by Jack Brocklebank and Harold Collinson, D.O. for Gloucestershire. They held meetings all over the large scattered rural division, covering some 600 square miles and 120 towns and villages. For three solid weeks they addressed meetings, some in the open air and others in large meeting rooms. At times Frank addressed as many as eleven meetings in a single day. On one occasion he held the platform at Boston Spa until 9-30 p.m. due to the late arrival of Bert from another meeting. On the eve of the poll he was at Micklefield with a room full of miners and Bert did not arrive until 10 p.m. As he stood there with sweat on his brow, wondering where Bert had got to, he heard a brass band in the distance and was informed that the miners from Garforth were carrying Bert shoulder high behind the band. Bert polled 24,352 votes, losing by only 116 votes. He should have won, but many voters had never voted before and in some villages many supporters did not vote because they refused to ride in the Tory cars. The problem of transport has always been a handicap in rural areas, as it is not permitted to hire cars to take electors to the polls, even if the candidate can afford it. However, Labour won an overwhelming victory, especially in the rural areas, where they took 50 seats from other parties. Norfolk North was won by Union President Alderman E.G. Gooch. So Labour came into power, inheriting all the difficulties of the transition from war to peace. They had to rebuild the bombed cities and towns, convert munitions and arms factories to peaceful uses once more, accommodate the millions of servicemen returning to civilian life, and build new roads, houses and sewers. The N.U.A.W. pressed for more and better housing for farm workers. Tom Williams became Minister of Agriculture in place of Mr. Hudson. His knowledge of farming and his sound judgement on all farming matters made him a popular choice. Development to the fullest extent in the home production of good food was the keyword and an atmosphere of confidence prevailed in agricultural circles.

It was not long, however, before the Union discovered that, although the need for food production was as great as ever, the regular labour force on the land was less than it had been the previous year. There were 7,000 fewer Land Army girls and 9,900 fewer workers. Casual workers were down too by some 3,000, while P.O.W.s employed on the land had increased by

Bert Hazell (left) presents Frank Robinson with a clock after 28½ years on the Executive Committee of the N.U.A.W., 1970. (Dennis J. Boyle)

almost 30,000. Due to the lifting of direction orders, there was a steep decline in the growing of wheat and potatoes, but an increase in barley, oats and mixed corn. Overall, however the acreage of grain was down on the previous year. Numbers of cattle were also less than the 10,000 head of the previous year. Both the National Farmers' Union (N.F.U.) and the N.U.A.W. were gravely concerned. General Secretary Alf Dann stated that it looked like a repetition of the days before the war and pointed out that if it had not been for workers being tied to the land the drift would have been greater.

It was about this time that Jack Davidson retired and Bob Stanley became D.O. for Northumberland. If agriculture was to retain its skilled workers and attract others, then their importance to the nation would have to be acknowledged and suitably rewarded. Wages and conditions comparable to those in towns would have to be introduced. The Government then gave a clear statement of crops and food required and put into operation an immediate release from the Forces of skilled farm workers. In the next few years conditions gradually improved. Housing was improved with the installation of electricity, better water supply and modern sanitation. Better schools and amenities such as village halls were also proposed. British farms became more mechanised, and the workers acquired new skills. The County Agricultural Executive Committee had greater powers to ensure efficient farming, and dispossession orders were served on badly-run farms. There is a saying that good comes out of evil, and, if the war did anything, it made the 'townies' realise the necessity of the agricultural communities. Food is not simply something to be bought in the shops, but something which has to be planned and worked for years ahead by farmers and farm-workers, under the 'direction' of the Government. The efforts made in those years immediately after the war secured maximum production using mechanisation, electrification, improved strains of seed, fertilizers, and up-to-date methods of livestock production, resulting in an agricultural industry of which the nation could be proud.

In 1946 elections were held for Parish Councils, County Councils and Rural District Councils. Parish Councils were in those days elected by a show of hands at the Parish Meeting, unless someone in the meeting demanded a poll. The law also provided that a County Council could, at the request of a Parish Council or Parish Meeting, direct that the Parish Councillors be elected by nomination and a poll taken instead of the show of hands. Frank stood as a candidate for the East Riding County Council, being narrowly defeated by Campbell Connor, a well-known stalwart in Eastern Holderness, who had a strong Labour following, although standing as an Independent. Frank was successful in being elected to the Holderness Rural District Council, however, and remained a member representing Patrington for 28 years, until local government reorganisation in 1974. He then served on the newly-formed Holderness District Council.

Chapter Ten

PEACETIME PROBLEMS

The year 1946 brought with it changes in the methods of British farming, many people subscribing to the view that the future of British agriculture lay in large-scale mechanised farms, in spite of the fact that 47% of holdings did not exceed 150 acres, and this figure did not take account of holdings of less than 5 acres. Land settlement schemes were set up to help alleviate the unemployment problem, but these were criticized in some quarters. No doubt many remembered similar schemes after the first war, when many ex-servicemen took smallholdings, but after years of hard drudgery had difficulty in paying off the loans they had received at the beginning. Smallholdings administered by the County Councils and rented to applicants with the necessary agricultural qualifications did prove successful, however, and Government land settlement schemes in different parts of the country also proved worthwhile. In these schemes, settlers pooled their products into a central store and did all their own buying and selling.

The 'tied' or service cottage on the farm was again a matter for debate. This was the system whereby the farmworker received a cottage in which to live as long as he worked on the farm. If he wanted to leave agriculture, however, he had no assets and nowhere to live. If his employment ended through old age, sickness, injury or dismissal, then he lost not only his livelihood but also his home. Unscrupulous farmers would use this as a sort of blackmail to keep the men in line. The farmers with few exceptions opposed any move to abolish the system, pointing out the need for stockmen, cowmen and other key workers to live near the farm. The Union argued that in the new, mechanised age transport and telephones were much improved, and many workers wished to live in the village communities and not be tied to a farm cottage. What they needed was a feeling of security instead of the threat of eviction hanging over their heads. The Government could not be persuaded to bring in a Bill for the abolition of the tied cottage, but local councils were urged to build more council houses, and grants were paid for those let to agricultural workers, who enjoyed the benefit of a reduced rental. In some areas even this system was exploited by the farmers. Some council houses were allocated to a certain farmer for the benefit of his workers, which meant that if any of them left that farmer's employ then pressure was brought to bear to evict him from his home, the house being allocated for an agricultural worker. This was taken up with the Ministry, and instructions were issued to the councils concerned that these men should not be forced to leave, but, if they were no longer employed in agriculture, then their rents would be adjusted accordingly.

The Holderness Council, on which Frank served, always acted fairly in this respect, and a large percentage of houses were let to workers in agriculture. When in later years the agricultural subsidy was removed, and all rents made equal, Frank supported this as he had always felt that to charge a lower rent to an agricultural worker made it easy to class him as inferior to others and did not give him the status which was his due as one of Britain's key workers.

In his capacity as an Executive member Frank was kept very busy addressing meetings in Cheshire, Flint, Durham and Northumberland, enrolling scores of new members. At Ashington there was a packed meeting with bus loads coming from nearby villages. The meeting, joined by M.P. Alf Robbins, finished with songs and dancing, showing again the hospitality of the Northumbrian people.

In July, 1946, farm workers' wages were increased to £4 per week for adult males and £3 for women, with overtime rates at 2/1d. per hour and 2/6d. at weekends. At the biennial conference held at Exeter, Frank moved the resolution on wages. While he welcomed the recommendation of the Agricultural Wages Board as a somewhat belated acknowledgment of the central part played in the national economy by land workers, both in peace and war, he emphasised that the wage now proposed fell short of the modest claim which had been so long before the Board, that of £4 10s., and this should have been granted in full. However, considering the grave world food situation, Frank stated that the Union had no wish to add to existing difficulties, and recommended that the offer should be accepted on the understanding that such partial satisfaction would not abrogate their claim which they intended to press with renewed energy at the opportune time. A long debate ensued with the usual criticism against the farmers and Wages Board for the attitude they had adopted towards the claim. Eventually the award, a ten shilling increase, was accepted.

A resolution that the Communist Party should be supported in its application to be affiliated to the Labour Party was, after a lengthy discussion, heavily defeated by 103 votes to 6. Frank was re-elected to represent the Northern Counties by a majority of almost 3,000.

The year 1947 began with one of the heaviest snowfalls ever known, with snowdrifts up to 20 feet deep and many villages completely cut off and isolated. Many people were without food and coal for weeks, and in the East

Yorkshire Wolds the R.A.F. came to their aid by dropping supplies. In Patrington, Frank had a seven-week battle against the weather, having to spend days digging the snow away in order to get into the coalyard at the station and to the coal cells. Even then it was only by hiring tractors and men from friendly farmers that he was able to make any deliveries. He would, of course, have preferred to sit at home and keep warm, but so many people were desperate for coal to keep warm that in spite of discomfort and financial loss he managed to keep a makeshift service going.

Following the great snow came disastrous floods and gales with great damage to property and losses to the farmers, many of whom had lost sheep and lambs which were suffocated in the snowdrifts. Reports from the National Farmers' Union showed that 1,370,000 sheep and lambs were lost as a result of snow, floods and exposure. 30,000 store cattle were lost, and 100,000 tons of potatoes ruined. Loss of calves, pigs and poultry cost half a million pounds, and some 364,000 acres of land were under water. Without doubt it was one of the greatest food production tragedies the country had ever known, and it was said to have caused more loss of food production than the whole of the war years. Farm houses and cottages were also badly affected, and the Union received stories from all over the country telling of walls, floors, carpets and furniture sodden and fouled by slime. Many families had had to flee from their homes, leaving everything to the mercy of the rushing waters.

The Government took urgent measures to meet the situation. Generous grants were given, and the Land Drainage Division of the Ministry of Agriculture, assisted by local authorities, the Army and the Navy, helped with the reclamation work. The Lord Mayor of London opened a National Flood Distress Fund with the approval of the Government, which contributed £1,000,000. It was a national effort, with contributions from the T.U.C. and the N.U.A.W., while the N.F.U. also opened an Agricultural Disaster Fund. Once again it was the farming communities of Britain who were up against it, but they fought and won through.

At this time there still remained a large number of German P.O.W.s in Britain and they were given high priority to work in agriculture and in the harvest fields. Arrangements were being considered by the Ministry of Labour for farmers to retain P.O.W.s on a civilian basis, providing that the farmers could provide accommodation without detriment to the British workers. This would mean, of course, that ex-P.O.W.s would then be entitled to the same wages as any other civilian. The Executive Committee of the N.U.A.W., meeting in London, after considering all the factors, passed a resolution that, while appreciating the great tasks which faced the labour force on British farms, and realising that employment of auxiliary labour at that time might be necessary, it was with regret that they learned of the statement concerning the retaining of P.O.W.s, a matter in which the Agricultural Workers' Union had not been consulted. The Union therefore urged the Government that, in matters concerning long term policy, the Union should be fully consulted and that the declared policy should be the return of all P.O.W.s to their own country. The Ministry and the Home Secretary, Mr. Chuter Ede, however, agreed to P.O.W.s staying as civilians if they so wished, unless there were good reasons for refusal, but this did not mean they could stay indefinitely. The situation in Germany made it difficult to send them all home. The towns and cities had sustained terrible damage and the people were going hungry, but in the countryside there seemed to be plenty of food. Hitler had for six years looted the foodstuffs of other countries and allowed the German farmers to grow what they liked. So, while the city dwellers went hungry, the country people had plenty of meat and poultry.

During 1947 the Tolpuddle Martyrs' celebration took place from 14 to 20 July. The Executive Committee and Head Office staff, together with the members from all the Dorset villages, took part, with bands and banners. On the Sunday, under the Martyrs' Tree at Tolpuddle, a service was held, followed by a parade through the village streets, headed by N.U.A.W. President Alderman E.G. Gooch, M.P., and Alf Dann, General Secretary, Dr. Hugh Dalton, Chancellor of the Exchequer, and the members of the Executive Committee. The story associated with the tiny Dorset village of Tolpuddle is enshrined in the history of the working class movement, and the words inscribed on the gateway erected at Tolpuddle should be an inspiration to our own and future generations.

The village was the home of six farm workers who were arrested, thrown into prison and, after a trial which was a travesty of justice, sentenced to be transported for seven years, with all its horrors of chain gangs and slave labour, because they dared to form a trade union with the object of resisting a reduction of wages to six shillings a week. They were all men of good character — honest, hard-working and reliable. Four of them were married with children. None were illiterate, all were Methodists, and five were local preachers. George Loveless, their leader, had organised them to claim decent wages and conditions for their wives and families in order to preserve them from utter degradation and starvation. When George Loveless was sentenced at the Dorchester Assizes in 1834, he asked for pencil and paper, and wrote these lines:

> 'God is our guide.
> No swords we draw.
> We kindle not world's battle fires.
> By reason, justice, union, law,
> We claim the birthright of our sires,
> We raise the watchword, liberty,
> We will, we will, we will be free.'

The procession on that Sunday in 1947 passed six cottages built by the Trade Union movement in the centenary year, 1938, each named after one of the six martyrs and let to retired farmworkers of the Union who had given yeoman service. They marched past the old cottage of George Loveless where the martyrs used to meet, and the chapel where they preached. Each year the names of these six brave men are remembered: George and James Loveless, Thomas and John Standfield, James Hammett and James Brine.

In August, 1947, farm wages were increased to £4 10s. per week after another hard struggle with the Wages Board, but lodging for men was valued at £1 10s., which was deducted from the wages of workers living in. It was also in 1947 that male agricultural workers born between 1 October and 31 December, 1929, were required to register for military service. The Union took up the case for the exemption of men in the main agricultural occupations who were regularly employed before the date of registration or who had entered full-time agricultural employment within three months of completing their education. Suspension of call-up was granted and the County Agricultural Executive Committee was able to certify *bona fide* workers whose retention was essential to food production. Any such men, however, who left agricultural employment became liable for call-up. Many remained in the agricultural industry in order to evade National Service, but after National Service ceased, many of them left agriculture.

At the Trades Union Congress at Southport that year, Frank moved on behalf of the N.U.A.W. a resolution urging wages comparable with those in skilled industry, houses with modern comforts and amenities, and security from the fear of eviction from tied cottages. He spoke of the importance of agriculture to the nation, even in times of peace, and the need for the production of more and more food. He paid tribute to the Women's Land Army, the conscientious objectors and prisoners-of-war, who had helped to keep the farms going in time of war. But in 1947, with the W.L.A. reduced from 70,000 to 20,000, the C.O.s having returned to their normal jobs, and the P.O.W.s gradually returning to their own countries, it was essential to build up a strong labour force in agriculture in order to reduce the gap between imports and exports. If the targets were to be reached, and a contented agricultural labour force was to be established, then a great recruitment of the right men was necessary. Frank agreed that machinery would play a great part in the future of British agriculture, but he reminded the conference that men were still masters of the machine. Brother Sid King of Lincolnshire seconded the resolution, deploring the use of school children on farms, which was detrimental to their education. The resolution received unanimous support.

1947 ended with the wedding of Princess Elizabeth to the Duke of Edinburgh at Westminster Abbey. Frank was in London at the time and was privileged to see the procession as it came down the Mall, with husband and wife looking radiantly happy after the ceremony. The Union also took part in the Lord Mayor's Parade in London, having a 60-foot trailer to display their exhibit which depicted rural housing, old and new.

Chapter Eleven

THE WORK CONTINUES

When Frank was again re-elected to the N.E.C. in 1948, he was joined by another Yorkshireman, Joss McCage from Rossington. Joss had taken an active part in trade union work over many years, having been a member of the N.U.A.W. since 1918. In 1922 he was victimised for his union activities and lost his job on the farm, but obtained work as a surface worker at the colliery, becoming a member not only of the N.U.A.W. but also the Yorkshire Miners' Association. He also served on his parish council and the Doncaster Rural District Council. Joss and Frank became good friends, and they spent many happy times together, often at Joss's home in Rossington. He only served on the N.E.C. for two years, but they remained friends for many years.

1948 also saw the Government White Paper on income and prices. Wage increases were therefore difficult to obtain, but increases were made within the terms of the White Paper. Some 23,000 German P.O.W.s were allowed to stay as civilians at their own request, and there were also some 8,000 Polish and 8,000 Ukrainians placed in agricultural jobs, mostly living in hostels. The Union was concerned at the number of British workers who were being lured away from agriculture and at the short-sightedness of some farmers who relied on foreign workers, both regular and casual, to augment their labour requirements. The drop of 11,000 in the intake of school leavers into agriculture was in the main due to the raising of the school-leaving age to 15, while exemption from military service helped the retention and recruitment of those eligible for call-up. The rural housing programme was being strongly urged, with more council houses available for farm workers. Further pressure was applied for the abolition of the tied cottage. It was not suggested that all farm cottages should be pulled down, but that, before a worker could be evicted, an order of the court should be obtained, and that, before any eviction was granted, suitable accommodation should be provided.

The Union's biennial conference was held at Scarborough, with some 200 delegates attending from all over the country. A real Yorkshire welcome was given to the delegates in spite of the food rationing which was still in force.

On the last day of the conference a coach trip over the moors was arranged. Among the many Yorkshire stalwarts of the Union was Billy Crawford, then 80 years of age, who had been the first Yorkshire Organiser in 1918. Bill Piercy of Marr, West Yorkshire, was a staunch Methodist and local preacher, who held the gold medal of the Union for long service. Ben Bassett of Sherburn, East Yorkshire, was another 1918 member, who had 19 children and played the organ at the Methodist Church. Zach Bemrose, the Patrington Branch Chairman, another Methodist local preacher, was a life-long trade unionist and ex-member of the N.E.C. Tom Gascoigne was an active member of the Yorkshire County Committee who was in charge of an agricultural hostel and had joined the Union in the war years. Harry Maulson of Bilton, East Yorkshire, was another Methodist local preacher and 1918 member, a great orator who had served ten years on the N.E.C. Then there were the three District Organisers: Bert Hazell, East Yorkshire, later to become an M.P. and President of the Union; Jack Brocklebank from East Yorkshire, D.O. for North Yorkshire; Wilf Sigsworth, West Yorkshire, appointed in 1945. It was a successful conference, and on Whit Sunday both Herbert Morrison, M.P., and Tom Williams, M.P., Minister of Agriculture, addressed the greatest rally of farm workers ever held in Yorkshire.

Later in 1948, Frank attended the International Landworkers' Federation (I.L.F.) held in Amsterdam. The hospitable and warm-hearted people of Holland gave them a truly great welcome. They had undergone terrible deprivations under the German occupation of their country, but in spite of rationing were determined to overcome their economic difficulties. The British delegation consisted of Edwin Gooch, M.P., President of the Union, with Frank and his three old friends, Tom Bavin, Hubert Luckett and Charlie Chandler. Dr. J.F. Duncan, President of the Scottish farm workers' union, presided over the conference, the first to be held following the war. The I.L.F. had been founded in Amsterdam in 1920. The conference was held in a fine hotel in the centre of the city, and the delegates were surprised to find the best room, a large double room with bathroom, reserved for Tom Bavin. Frank requested to be allowed to share the room with him. Having obtained Tom's permission, Frank moved from his single room to share the most palatial room in the hotel. The President next morning complained of only having a single room, and could not understand why. It was only later in the week that it was discovered that Tom had been mistaken for another distinguished English gentleman.

Many important decisions had to be made, to place the finances on a firm footing once more so that the work of the I.L.F. could progress. There were many problems with foreign labour in the various countries after the German occupation during the war. Naturally there was still a feeling of suspicion, but the British delegation, mindful of the many German P.O.W.s in England still working on the farms, decided that the

Farmworkers' Union in the British Zone of Germany should be re-admitted to the Federation. They also pressed for direct representation of farm workers on the Food and Agricultural Organisation (F.A.O.) of the United Nations and on the Permanent Agricultural Committee of the International Labour Organisation (I.L.O.) They decided, however, not to join the World Federation of Trade Unions (W.F.T.U.)

They heard and learned a lot about the people of Holland during their stay, and all fell in love with the beautiful city of Amsterdam, the 'Venice of the North', with its 70 museums and collections, two universities, 50 canals, 400 bridges and 4,000 ancient buildings and monuments. The Dutch landworkers' union organised a trip along the canals by motor launch, and they visited the Zuider Zee country to see the transformation which had taken place following the breaching of the bank by Hitler's troops, causing the flooding of thousands of acres of valuable land previously reclaimed from the sea.

On the way home, an incident occurred in the Customs hall at Harwich. As they presented their luggage for inspection, the Customs officer eyed Charlie Chandler's portly frame and asked, 'Is that your tummy?' Having convinced themselves that it was, and that Charlie had no valuable articles hidden around his middle, the party was allowed to proceed.

July 5, 1948 saw the implementation of the Beveridge Report, the introduction of Social Security, beginning the great uphill struggle to eradicate the poverty which existed in thousands of homes throughout Britain. Frank went to pay his regular quarterly doctor's bill for attendance to his wife and family.

'It is with a feeling of joy,' he said, 'that I come to pay your bill.'

'Thanks,' he replied. 'I wish others had the same willingness.'

Frank then reminded him that, thanks to the N.H.S., it was the last he would have to pay, and expressed the hope that the Welfare State would achieve its aims of providing security in adversity for every man, woman and child.

The Royal Agricultural Show was held at York that year, and the Union had a large, attractive marquee. Frank was in charge of the Information Centre and during the week enrolled many new members from all over the country. Among the visitors were delegates from the U.S.A., Australia, New Zealand, Sweden, Denmark, Eire, Czechoslovakia and other countries.

Since the great snow-fall of 1947, Frank had found it arduous to run his coal business. His eldest son had decided to join the armed forces, and with the advent of electricity and central heating, and the big coal-dealers with their large lorries able to bring in coal much cheaper, Frank decided to sell up and concentrate on his small agricultural holding. This would enable him to assist the local farmers on a casual basis and give more time to Union affairs, both nationally and internationally. The coal business was sold to a young man who had served in the Navy. Frank later had an illness which lasted 3 or 4 months, during which Zach Bemrose and a neighbouring farmer supervised his harvest, cutting, leading and threshing 4 acres of oats, which yielded over 12 quarters to the acre.

A bitter struggle took place that year regarding the the application by the Communist Party to be affiliated to the Trade Union movement. The T.U.C. case against was that members of the Communist Party were not free to express their own opinions, but were expected to put into operation a policy determined outside the machinery of their own national party and dictated from elsewhere. There were also fears that attempts would be made to project that policy into the T.U.C. by means far outside the normal democratic procedures. The N.U.A.W. had members who were known to be Communists. Jack Dunman, editor of the *County Standard*, had served the Union well, being a prominent and able speaker. He and another Communist, Wilf Willett of Kent, attracted many farm workers to the Union through their Communist literature and their articles in the *County Standard* and the *Daily Worker*, which they supplied freely at Union conferences. They did their best to persuade farm workers to join the Communist Party, travelling all over the country to spread their philosophy. They did excellent work for farm workers, but never succeeded in enlisting much support for the Communist Party. Free thought, free discussion, free assembly, free worship and a free press are priceless possessions, but they are not part of Communist philosophy, and the British working man should always remember this. Both Jack Dunman and Wilf Willett have since died, and Frank always considered them friends, for they never bore a grudge when defeated.

Frank Robinson (left) with his twin brother, Tom.

Chapter Twelve

INTO THE FIFTIES

By 1949 the union had managed to obtain wages of £4 14s. per week, with a reduction of hours to 47, but farmworkers were still below the standard of other major industrial workers. Rationing of food was still in force, and housewives had to eke out a meat ration of 1s. 4d., with a few more sausage and meat pies being offered. Frank was still kept very busy; in addition to his Union work and service on both the Rural District Council and Parish Council, he was honorary fixture secretary for the local cricket club and secretary of the South Holderness Association Football League.

In 1950, the Control of Engagement Order was removed, which had given exemption from National Service to those occupied in agriculture and mining. This meant that workers who now left the farming industry could be directed into other work of national importance or called up into H.M. Forces. This was watched carefully by the Union, for there was no doubt that many had stayed in farming despite the low wages to escape being called up, and these men were used as a lever when negotiating wages.

In the 1950 general election, N.U.A.W. President Edwin Gooch successfully fought to retain his North Norfolk seat. Other members of the N.U.A.W. who contested the election were Bert Hazell in Barkston Ash, Billy Case in Salisbury and Eddy Jones in Leominster. None of them were successful, and, although Labour won the election, their majority was much reduced.

Tom Williams, Minister of Agriculture, addressed the Union's biennial conference at Margate, speaking on the two-year expansion programme for agriculture. He praised both farmers and farm workers and stated that the provisions of the Agriculture Act gave farm workers an important part in the self-government of the industry through the County Agricultural Executive Committees. Speaking about tied cottages, the Minister said that he appreciated the problem but had little power to do anything about it. This caused ironic laughter in several parts of the hall. He did promise to discuss the matter with the N.F.U. and with the Minister of Health and Housing. Moving the resolution on weed-killers, Frank stated how seriously perturbed the farm workers were at the totally inadequate attempts made to deal with the growing menace of poisonous substances in agriculture. Quoting several cases of poisoning, some of which had proved fatal, he urged the Minister to compel safety regulations and compulsory medical supervision. He also urged the Home Secretary to ban the use of substances such as D.N.O.C. (dinitro-orthocresol) and Parathion, both in use as crop sprays, yet deadly to men, five deaths already having occurred in Britain. After some discussion, the resolution was passed unanimously.

In July a delegation travelled to Zurich for the I.L.F. conference. Frank was again included, along with Edwin Gooch, J. Barsby, Bert Huson and B. Leeder, plus Dr. J.F. Duncan and Alex Evans from Scotland. The conference was held at the magnificent headquarters of the Swiss Workers' Union, with the majestic Alps and lovely lake adding to the beauty of the surroundings. They were given a very warm welcome, and the admirably planned city with its grand cathedral, fine churches, elegant modern buildings, large hotels and wide, clean streets greatly impressed everyone. Altogether over a dozen European countries had sent delegations, and it was pleasing that Germany was once again represented after an absence of 18 years, due to Hitler's suppression of the trade unions in the pre-war years. Also present were representations from the International Confederation of Free Trade Unions (I.C.F.T.U.), I.L.O. and F.A.O. Many matters were discussed concerning the work of land workers everywhere. Adri de Ruigte, Secretary of the Dutch land workers, the oldest land workers' association in Europe, who took part in the founding of the I.L.F. in 1920, was an able Secretary. Edwin Gooch was elected President to replace Dr. Duncan, who was retiring after 26 years as President. In addition to conference work, the delegates enjoyed a trip down the lake and an excellent dinner, with entertainment consisting of a young lady with a guitar and yodelling songs. They could look down from the mountain heights to the twinkling lights of night-time Zurich.

1950 brought to an end the Women's Land Army which had contributed so much hard work through the difficult years. The W.L.A., formed in 1939, took some time to find recognition; at first few farmers wanted them, but in time they came to respect the wearers of the familiar green uniform. What the farm workers thought when these pale-faced lasses came among them is better not stated, but soon they too grew to respect and admire them, for, whether driving horses or ploughing, milking or feeding stock, haymaking or forking the sheaves, or even pulling mangels or turnips, they did a magnificent job. Many of them stayed on the land and became the wives of farmers and farm workers. They did much to bring town and country together and helped to prevent the hunger which threatened.

In 1951 Frank was again re-elected to the N.E.C. with an overall majority over five other contenders. In February he was away campaigning in Cornwall. They had some excellent meetings and many new members were enrolled. Frank made many new friends, including F. Cole, the District

Organiser, and Garfield Mitchell who was a member of the Cornish Male Voice Choir and holder of the R.S.P.C.A medal and a certificate for life-saving. Concern about the drift from the land to more remunerative employment and the call-up of farm workers to National Service was causing concern throughout the country, and, when up in Northumberland and Durham, Frank learned that some 1,000 workers had left the land. Resolutions were passed for at least £6 per week, for it was felt that, unless adequate wages were paid, the drift would continue and conditions would act as a deterrent to the agricultural industry. Bob Stanley the D.O. and Frank addressed crowded meetings at Cramlington, Shankhouse, Seaton and Morpeth during a busy weekend.

In July Frank went by air to the Swedish Landworkers' Congress at Stockholm to convey the fraternal greetings of the Union. He recalled with joy and pride the warm-hearted generosity and friendliness of the Swedish people in that lovely city set in a beautiful country. The Swedish Union held a congress every five years, the last having been in 1946. Sweden is a comparatively small country, and the Union had around 45,000 members. The congress was held in the magnificent Great Concert Hall of Stockholm. There were about 300 delegates and in addition officers of the Union, the Minister of Agriculture, Gunnar Strang, and Labour Minister, Ivan Anderson. The eight tiers of the concert hall were filled with the wives of Union officials and delegates, and members of the public. Magnificent begonias, calceolarias and other blooms beautified the platform and the gangways. Banners from all the districts of Sweden, with the national banner in the centre, formed a striking and colourful background to the platform. The national flags of the countries represented floated overhead, among them the Union Jack, which made Frank realise the importance of his role as Britain's sole representative. The congress met every day from 9-30 a.m. to 1 p.m. and from 3 p.m. until 7 p.m. The problems of the Swedish land-workers were similar to those of Britain — wages and prices, rises in the cost of living, unemployment, education, Union membership, *etc.* Each day, representatives of the

Frank Robinson speaking in Stockholm, 1951.

other countries were called upon to give their fraternal greetings, the honour falling to Frank on the third day. Very conscious of his responsibility, he compared the conditions in their respective countries, and stressed their aspirations for the future. He did not forget the contribution made by the early Union pioneers, and referred to the transformation of the agricultural industry in recent years by mechanisation and stressed the supreme importance of land and forestry workers in supplying the things they most urgently needed. He also referred to the I.L.F. which the Swedish Union had helped to form. The first to congratulate him afterwards was Gunnar Strang. He and his wife Ingrid later visited England and Frank had the pleasure of meeting them again with Tom Williams, Britain's Minister of Agriculture. During the congress, Frank was partnered one evening by English strong girl June Rhodes, who bent iron bars and easily tore large volumes in half. Frank found the Scandinavians very friendly and they always welcomed him to their country on later visits.

It was also in 1951 that a train load of Union members paid a visit to the Festival of Britain in London, 425 members and their wives going from the East Riding alone. They set off at 10-30 p.m., meeting up with other members on the way, and arrived in London at 5-40 a.m. Some fourteen buses were needed to convey members around London. A visit was also made to Windsor and Hampton Court, before visiting the Exhibition in the afternoon. In the evening they found their own entertainment, many visiting the theatre. Leaving London around midnight, they arrived home on Sunday morning and fell into bed.

1951 saw the defeat of the Labour government, surrendering office after six difficult years in the immediate post-war period. Edwin Gooch retained his seat in North Norfolk, but the Liberals were heavily defeated; out of 109 Liberal candidates, only half a dozen were elected, and all ten Communist candidates lost their deposits. The Labour vote in total was higher than that of the Conservatives, but, as the Tories obtained more seats, they were considered to have won the election. It remained to be seen how they would adapt to the economic structure erected by Labour in those critical six years.

Chapter Thirteen
A TIME OF LOSS

The year 1952 took Frank to Northumberland once more to visit his many friends — Jack Short at Chathill, Bob Kerr at Morpeth, J. Archibold and J. Makepiece at Alnwick, and Bob Stanley, the D.O., and his wife in the colliery village of Waddington. Everywhere he received the kind welcome and warm hospitality typical of the Geordies. Those people more used to the soft landscape of the South of England are not aware of the stern, lonely beauty of the North until they pay it a visit. The basis of the agriculture was sheep and cattle farming, and in many places it was very isolated, but Frank found it a joy to be among the warmth and humour of the farm workers.

The deepening economic crisis made it all the more important that food production should increase, and farmers increased their demands for better prices while their workers continued their claims for more wages.

In May Frank was again included in the delegation to the I.L.F., which was held that year in Salzburg, Austria. After a beautiful journey by rail across France and Switzerland and over the Alps to Austria, they were welcomed to the beautiful city of Salzburg by the Deputy Governor of the province, the Mayor of the city and the General Secretary of the Austrian labour movement. Delegates from over 20 countries were present in addition to members of many United Nations Organisations. The congress was mainly concerned with the problems of the world's plantation workers. The delegates were also taken round the beauties of the scenery, visiting the waterfalls and national parks, travelling over the Gross Glockner alpine road, wondering at the cable railways, and gasping at the breathtaking beauty of the villages such as Bad Hofgastein. They had lunch at Salzburg Castle and visited the house of Mozart and the beautiful Church of St. Peter's during their stay.

Later in May Frank attended the Union's conference at Skegness, with some 200 delegates present. A wage of £7 per week was urged, and a scathing attack was made on the tied cottage system. Other matters dealt with included housing, education, safety and agricultural production. Frank then spent a week with Bro. Clark, the D.O. for Hereford and Monmouth, campaigning and sorting out difficult matters in the area.

Afterwards he went on to spend a week with the D.O. for Lancashire. The East Riding members, following the success of the outing to the Festival of Britain the previous year, persuaded their D.O., Bert Hazell, to organise another outing, this time to Bonnie Scotland.

The annual Durham Miners' Gala in July was attended by Aneurin Bevan, Sir William Lowther, Sir Hartley Shawcross and other well-known trade union leaders. This gala, virtually unknown in the Southern counties, was one of the most exuberant events in the country. Early in the morning one was awoken by the sound of brass bands leading the miners' lodges, with banners flying, through the streets to Durham Racecourse. Some 350,000 converged on Durham, gaily dressed, singing and dancing as they accompanied the miners. From all over Durham and beyond they came, packing the streets chock-a-block; the mounted police did an excellent job in controlling the crowds and keeping the way open for the marching miners. Some of the banners were draped with black, a sign that some miners had lost their lives underground since the last Gala day. Beer flowed in a glorious confusion of jugs, bottles, paper hats, balloons, youngsters kissing and flirting, big wheel, bingo, waltzers, boxing booths, fat men, little men, and trade union leaders on platforms shouting out their well-prepared speeches. In the evening, the contingent from the N.U.A.W. attended a miners' meeting, supper and concert, where Frank had the honour of giving the toast to the miners. Over the years Frank attended many of these events, and never forgot the speakers such as Nye Bevan, Hugh Gaitskell, and miners' leaders Will Lowther and Sam Watson. Each year the event was followed by a service in Durham Cathedral, attended by 3,000 or more and accompanied by the massed bands, another unforgettable experience.

In September and October Frank represented the I.L.F. at the 'Green Pool' conference in Brussels. He went with General Secretary Alf Dann, who was representing the T.U.C. Alf was not well, and on one occasion Frank found him very ill in his room. He fought it off, however, and apparently recovered quickly. The purpose of the conference was to discuss European agriculture and the pooling of all European food production in one common market. The British delegates, because of the agreements with Commonwealth countries, could not enter into any new agreements without consultation with the Government, but hopes were expressed that some ways might be found to bring about a more close association with the Europeans. Mr. Nutting, the Under Secretary for Foreign Affairs, said that his government were certainly interested in any proposals which would produce more food in Europe and reduce our dollar dependence on overseas markets. It was agreed that further discussions and clarification of technical details were necessary before any clear conclusions could be drawn. In speaking at the conference, Frank urged co-operation rather than integration. The position of plantation workers was again raised, and a committee was set up to deal with this problem, financed for one year by the I.C.F.T.U. Frank put forward the name of Tom Bavin, his ex-N.E.C. colleague from Lincolnshire. Tom was contacted by telephone, interviewed in Brussels, and later became General Secretary of the International Federation of Plantation and Allied Workers (I.F.P.A.W.) whose headquarters were in Geneva.

At the end of the year Frank spent a week in Cheshire addressing large meetings of 200 to 300 strong. 1953 commenced with a great shock, the death of Alf Dann, the Union's General Secretary, at the age of 59. Dann, as he was always known, was a Londoner who came into contact with the Union through helping on the land while serving with H.M. Forces in the 1914-18 war. A solicitor by profession, he applied for a job with the Union's legal department in London, and in 1919 he took charge of that office in Gray's Inn Road. Devoted to his work, he served the Union and the farm workers well, being elected General Secretary on the retirement of William Holmes in 1944. He was immensely sincere and lived for the Union, being engaged on Union work when he collapsed. Frank served with him from 1952, both abroad and at home. He drove himself to work, was temperamental in many ways, hard-hitting at times, but honest. Even those who disagreed with him respected him for his forthright views devoid of any fancy tricks of oratory, always saying exactly what he meant. Tributes poured in to Head Office from the T.U.C., N.F.U., International Committee and Labour Party members.

1953 also brought great damage and loss as floods lashed the East Coast with unusual ferocity. Thousands of acres from Canvey Island and Foulness in Essex to Easington, Spurn, and further north were flooded. Farmsteads and livestock were swept away and homes had to be evacuated. In Holland more than 300,000 acres were flooded.

In May, Harold Collinson, head of the legal department, and one time D.O. for Gloucester, was elected as the new General Secretary. He and his wife Ivy soon became well known as they set about their long and arduous duties with a spirit of enthusiasm. Between N.E.C. meetings in London and work at home on the Rural District Council, Frank attended one-week campaigns in Shropshire, Wales and Cornwall, as well as dinners and social functions in his own area. At Relubbus in Cornwall he again visited Garfield Mitchell to find that his wife had broken her leg in the milking shed. Asking if she was a Union member, he was reminded with a smile that he had in fact paid her subscription for a while in return for hospitality. The Agricultural Wages Board was persuaded to allow £6 per week as the national minimum wage, the first major wage claim in the new General Secretary's term of office. Frank observed that Harold would make a good leader and negotiator. The year's activities included the East Riding members' outing, this time to Wales, the T.U.C. Conference, the Labour Party Conference and the annual Tolpuddle celebration in Dorset.

The Union activities continued through 1954. Edwin Gooch again raised the question of tied cottages in the House of Commons, but without success. Arthur Holmes, editor of *The Landworker,* the Union's monthly journal, retired after 35 years as an Organiser, the last 14 as Editor. A Methodist local preacher in his early days, he was a conscientious objector in the first war, appearing before a tribunal and offering for ambulance work. The colonel, however, finding that Arthur had some knowledge of agriculture, assigned him to work on the land. He became D.O. for East Kent, enrolling some 3,000 members as he travelled around on his bicycle. He was a confirmed bachelor and never had time for romance. On one occasion he took a girl to the pictures, forgot she was there, and walked out and left her. He was an avid reader with a thirst for knowledge, politics, religion and philosophy. Frank, who spent much time with him, shared rooms with him, and heard him lecture on many subjects, was very sorry to see him retire. He was awarded the M.B.E. in 1952. The Union's 1954 conference was held at Cheltenham, dealing with some 500 motions covering wages, rural housing, tied cottages, forestry workers, County Council roadmen and agricultural apprenticeships. Having campaigned in Gloucestershire several times, Frank was pleased to see old friends and be with Jim Paull of the N.E.C. on his native heath. At the end of the year the sad news was received of the death of Billy Crawford, the first Yorkshire D.O. in 1918, who passed away at the age of 87.

In January, 1955, the new wage of £6 7s. came into operation, overtime rate being 4s. 1d. per hour. Strong pressure was brought to bear in the House of Commons by Edwin Gooch and other M.P.s for implementation of the recommendations of the Gowers Committee Report which dealt with legislation for accident prevention in agriculture and buildings, the Union pressing for the same safeguards that were found in factories. The re-rating of industrial and agricultural land also came under scrutiny that year. Many argued that farmers' incomes were such that they could well afford to pay rates which would help the overburdened ratepayers, but the Union felt that to saddle farmers with an extra financial burden would not help the workers in their claim for higher wages. While it would increase the income of many of the local authorities, it would also increase the cost of food, for naturally the farmers would seek higher prices. The matter was left as before, with no pressure for the re-rating of agricultural land and buildings.

In May, 1955, the general election saw the return of the Conservative government with a comfortable majority, but two Union members, Edwin Gooch and Sidney Dye, were returned as Labour M.P.s for Norfolk. The Union again pressed for wages of £7 per week, but the decision was deferred until December when an increase of 8s. per week was given, making the wage £6 15s. At Margate the Labour Party Conference elected Edwin Gooch as Chairman for the coming year. The Wages Board decision not to allow the full award cast a gloom over Christmas and protests were heard throughout the country.

The new year opened with a barrage of criticism in the press about the inadequacy of the farm workers' pay award. Up and down the country protests continued, and the Wages Board was asked to think again. The drift of workers away from the land had increased dramatically, over 26,000 having left in the previous twelve months, the greatest number since 1948. Members throughout the country urged the N.E.C. to send a deputation to see Minister of Agriculture, D. Heathcote Amery, and Parliamentary Secretary, Robert Carr. The deputation consisted of six men — President Edwin Gooch, General Secretary, Harold Collinson, Billy Case, Frank, Percy Wells, M.P. and Tom Healy of the G.T.W.U. Agricultural Section. They met the Minister and expressed their discontent, urging for the T.U.C. to be represented on the Agricultural Wages Board. They also stated that they wished agriculture to play its full part in the national economy and expressed concern at the drift of workers from the land. At the end of the two-hour meeting the Minister promised to give consideration to the views expressed. Later that year the national minimum wage was raised to £7 1s.

1956 was a jubilee year for the Union, for it had been formed in 1906 by George Edwards at North Walsham in Norfolk and moved to London in 1918. Anyone interested in the early days of the Union should read *From Crow-scaring to Westminster*, the autobiography of George Edwards, and *Sharpen the Sickle* by Reg Groves, which tells the story of the N.U.A.W. from Tolpuddle days to the 1940s. The Union's biennial conference at Yarmouth in the county of its birth was naturally a time of celebration. It was opened by a demonstration on the Sunday, when 3,000 members and their wives marched in a parade which ran the whole length of Yarmouth's main shopping streets. The national banner, accompanied by banners from all over the country, was in the parade, and bands played all the way to the marina on the sea front. Frank was reminded of the Durham Miners' Gala. They assembled at the marina, where the main speaker was Hugh Gaitskell, followed by other M.P.s and trade union leaders, including Harold Collinson and Edwin Gooch, who presided. During the week the pioneers of the Union were honoured, and a visit was paid to the grave of George Edwards, where a short ceremony took place. Among the many important matters discussed at the conference were, of course, wages, tied cottages, accident and safety legislation, cost of living, National Service, council housing and agricultural policy.

1956 closed with another sad loss for the East Yorkshire area of the Union. Harry Maulson of Bilton died suddenly at the age of 73 after seemingly recovering from an operation. He had joined the Union when it was first formed in 1918 and was known throughout the East Riding for his oratory and fighting spirit. He had a great knowledge of agriculture and served on many agricultural committees. He later became a councillor and a magistrate. He served on the N.E.C. for ten years and was one of the

Union's trustees. He had intended to attend the golden jubilee conference but was prevented by his illness. He was the holder of the Union's gold badge and had been awarded the M.B.E. in the 1956 New Year Honours List. He was to Frank a faithful friend of long standing and was a loss not only to Yorkshire but also to a much wider field.

Frank Robinson chats to Edward Heath (later Prime Minister, at this time [1964] President of the Board of Trade) at a conference in Hull.

Chapter Fourteen

STUDY CONFERENCE

The Duke of Edinburgh's Study Conference took place at Oxford in July, 1956. It had taken three years in planning, and Frank found it one of the highlights and most interesting events in his life. Without the Duke of Edinburgh there would have been no conference; he alone had the prestige to bring it about, and the necessary tact, skill and patience to make a reality of an idea, with the help of that remarkable scientist, industrialist and administrator, Sir Harold Hartley, F.R.S. The conference brought together, from all over the Commonwealth, 280 men and women (in those days of sexual inequality, only a few women) who were engaged in the day-to-day tasks of industry and occupied, or were likely to occupy in the future, positions of responsibility within their industry. Frank, of course, was an agricultural delegate. For three weeks these people from immensely varied backgrounds mixed together and set out to study the human problems which they, by their decisions, would be affecting. They arrived on a special train which brought them from Paddington to Oxford on the afternoon of Sunday, 8 July. Having been allocated living quarters in the Colleges of Christ Church, Oriel and Pembroke, they met together for dinner in the College where they were to live. Frank was in 'E' Group, quartered in Christ Church.

The Duke of Edinburgh opened the conference at the Sheldonian Theatre, Oxford on Monday, 9 July. Speeches of welcome were given by the Right Honourable the Earl of Halifax and Alderman W.J. Allaway, Mayor of Oxford. After the ceremony, the delegates walked to Rhodes House, where the Group Chairman introduced each member to the Duke. That night the opening Conference Dinner took place in the grand dining hall of Christ Church. It was a splendid occasion: long polished tables, wines, silver plates, huge paintings and portraits on the walls. Here the whole conference and high dignitaries sat, with the Duke of Edinburgh presiding. Many of the delegates were awed by the setting and the occasion itself. Speeches were brief, and in proposing the toast to Her Majesty the Queen, the Duke said it was the first time he had been in a position to propose a toast to his own wife.

For the first four days, the conference heard a number of speakers who introduced the problems caused by the impact of industrialisation and the human problems of industry. These sessions, held at Rhodes House under the presidency of the Duke, were followed by discussions. For the next nine days the conference split into 20 groups, each group spending its time partly in an industrial centre and partly in London. For the final week the conference reassembled at Oxford and each group reported on its observations, with discussion following. The chairman of Group 'E', to which Frank was assigned, was Michael Clapham (later Sir Michael), who was to become the President of the Confederation of British Industry (C.B.I.) in 1974, and who was Managing Director of I.C.I. Ltd. The group of fourteen soon became friends and worked as a team. They were on Christian name terms, even the President being called Prince Philip.

On Thursday, 12 July, they left Oxford in a special coach which took them to the Green Park Hotel in London. During the afternoon they were guests at the garden party at Buckingham Palace. They were met by the Duke and introduced individually to Her Majesty the Queen, the Queen Mother, Princess Margaret and Princess Alexandra. In the evening they went to Shell-Mex House to be shown a film, *The Three Rivers*, about the Tees, Tyne and Wear, then finished the day with a visit to the *Prospect of Whitby*, a riverside tavern in Wapping Old Stairs, for a buffet supper and a sing-song.

While staying in London, Frank's group went down the sewers, wading thigh deep in the smelly darkness in order to learn first hand about the working conditions and the relationships between workers and management. Into this vast network beneath the streets of the capital was discharged the domestic waste, trade waste and rainwater from the whole of London and parts of the neighbouring counties of Middlesex, Essex, Surrey and Kent, an area of over 179 square miles with a resident population of some five million, though, of course, used by many more people during the working day. Flow was directed to the main sewers to be conveyed to one or other of the purification works on the banks of the Thames, east of the main city. This vast system of over 400 miles of main sewer was operated and maintained by more than 1,000 men. For administrative purposes, the main area was divided into two districts, North and South of the Thames, each district being sub-divided into four sub-districts, making eight in all. Each sub-district had its own depot, consisting of offices, stores, workshops, messes, ablutions, clothes-drying rooms, *etc*. Most of these depots had shower baths, and provisions were being made to install them at the depots still lacking.

The visiting group assembled at one of these depots, stripped off and donned stockings, dungarees, smocks, gloves and rubber thigh boots with studded leather soles. They were then taken to a man-hole near Lancaster House, where they climbed down a steep iron ladder into the main sewer, as large as the underground railway tunnels, and waded thigh deep through the sewage. Electric lights were fixed along the roofs for some distance, and a man was stationed above ground (the regular practice) to give warning of rain storms to the men underground. There was a danger of explosion from the methane gas formed in the sewers, and of disease being contracted from the rats which infested the sewers, particularly through abrasions to the skin, and every man carried a card with instructions in first aid. Beside Frank was D. Lee, managing director of a textile mill in Singapore, who was afraid to leave the ladder and clung to Frank like a leech. As he was only five feet tall, Frank could understand his uneasiness. After the visit below ground, they returned to the depot, had a good wash and shower, then assembled in the conference room where they were shown a film on the history of the London sewers. It was sobering to think that 100 years before, due to lack of sanitation, thousands had died of cholera, typhoid and other epidemics. Mr. E. A. Henderson, the Chief Engineer, said that the sewerman's job might appear to be an unenviable one, but many of the men had worked in the sewers for a long time and were reasonably content with their lot. They had a good relationship with the management, who were genuinely concerned for the men's welfare. Wages in 1956 for a 45-hour week, worked in shifts, was from £9 8s. 4d. to £9 18s. 4d. per week, with one fifth extra for night work. The men travelled to work in suits, collars and ties, changed into their overalls, left them in the drying sheds and returned home dressed as they came — who could tell if they were sewermen?

While in London, the group also visited the Dorchester Hotel where, after an introductory talk by Assistant Manager H.G. Davies, they made a tour of the hotel with its luxurious rooms and in the kitchens talked with some of the 800 staff. Lunch was given to the ten groups still in London at County Hall, where they were welcomed by the Chairman of the London County Council, Mrs. Helen C. Bentwick J.P. and Sir Harold Hartley. The afternoon was allowed as free time, and many members went to the theatre to see *The Pyjama Game*.

At 11-35 p.m. they departed by sleeper train from King's Cross for a night journey to Newcastle-upon-Tyne, arriving in time for breakfast at the Royal Station Hotel and a meeting with the press. At 9-15 a.m. they departed by bus for Vickers-Armstrong-Whitworth's shipbuilding yard. After an introductory talk, they were divided into four parties and guided around the production shop, welding shop, ship-fitters and joiners' shop. This was followed by lunch with the Joint Advisory Council and a session of questions and answers with the management. The total labour force was about 3,400, with an average of six vessels being completed annually; high class passenger vessels, cargo vessels and warships. In the afternoon the group visited C. A. Parsons and Co. Ltd., a firm founded in 1889 by Sir Charles Parsons for the development and manufacture of steam turbine plants. They were shown the foundry and apprentice school, and met the foremen and shop stewards who represented the 6,500 employees on the 55-acre site. After tea and a final discussion with the management, the group returned to the Royal Station Hotel to meet members of the Regional Board for Industry and the T.U.C. Regional Advisory Committee. Sir Mark Hodgson, O.B.E., Chairman of the Regional Board, took the chair. Frank had met many of the members before, during his trade union work, and among them was Bob Stanley, the N.U.A.W. Organiser for Northumberland. After dinner they had a good night's rest so that they would be ready early next morning to set off for Jarrow.

At Jarrow they were greeted at the Town Hall by Council Chairman Alderman G. A. Rose. After the usual introductory talks they were taken on a bus tour of Jarrow to see the old and new industries and housing. After discussion with the Mayor over coffee at the Town Hall, they travelled by launch to Corporation Quay at Newcastle, then on for lunch at the Mansion House with the Lord Mayor of Newcastle. They later visited the offices of Thomas Headley and Co. at Gosport and had dinner by invitation of Thomas Headley. This was presided over by Brigadier G. H. Walton, C.B., C.B.E., and many V.I.P.s and officials were present.

On the Sunday they attended a service in Durham Cathedral conducted by the Bishop of Durham. They had lunch in Durham Castle by kind permission of Durham College, and were taken around the Cathedral and Castle. They were then taken by bus to Otterburn for dinner at the Otterburn Tower Hotel with farmers and local government officers present. Frank was on familiar ground, as he had often visited Otterburn, and he enjoyed meeting many former friends once more.

Next morning they left at 8-30 a.m. to visit the Watergate and Morrison Busty collieries, which produced first class coking coal. The group divided into two, Frank's half visiting the Watergate Colliery. They stripped and dressed in miners' clothes, helmet and lamp, *etc.*, then descended in lifts 800 feet below the surface, and then rode in trucks to the coal face. The mine was fully mechanised and electrified. They observed the men shot-firing and putting the coal onto conveyor belts to be carried to the trucks and thence by lifts to the surface. Frank was very impressed, and said no one should begrudge the wages paid to the men at the coal face. After a shower at the pit head baths, they had lunch at the South Moor Club with members and officials of the Stanley Urban District Council and the National Coal Board. In the afternoon they visited Ransome and Mailes Bearing Co. Ltd., being welcomed by the manager, Mr. F.D. Graham, and given a tour of the factory. They were able to talk with management and workers after tea. Frank was asked to give a vote of thanks, and, having read that the firm was founded in 1906, he was able to congratulate them on having reached their golden jubilee year. Dinner at the Station Hotel was followed by a discussion group attended by the Regional Controller from the Ministry of Labour and National Service, Mr. W. G. Fuller, members of the Board of

Trade and Ministry of Supply, the Chairman of the Durham N.C.B., Mr. D. Skinner, and the Secretary of the Durham Associated Mineworkers' Union, Sam Watson, C.B.E.

Next day the group toured the Team Valley Estate in Gateshead, the first Government-sponsored organisation of its kind in Britain. Formed in 1936, it had developed into a 700-acre site employing some 12,500 people. Factories were let to industry on commercial leases usually of 21 years duration. Later the group split into three parties. Frank's party visited Short Bros. shipwrights, while the others visited Sir James Laing and Sons Ltd. and William Doxford and Sons Ltd. Around 4 p.m. the group reassembled to tour the new town of Peterlee on the coast midway between the Tees and the Wear. Planned to centralise development within a scattered rural district, the town was to provide housing for 30,000 people, and employment for those not engaged in mining, with a commercial centre to serve the district as a whole. The building of the town had commenced in 1951, and by 1956 2,400 houses had been completed and 8,000 people accommodated. Seventeen shops had been built and two primary schools opened. The first phase of a Technical College and secondary modern school were under construction. Two factories were being built and work had started on more shops and a church. The group returned to the Station Hotel for dinner, and left on the sleeper train at 10-35 p.m. to return to London. They arrived at 7-30 a.m. and returned to the Green Park Hotel. At 9-30 a.m., after a wash and brush up, they were at the British Transport Headquarters for a short address by the Chairman, General Sir Brian Robertson, and a talk by Major General L. Wansbrough Jones. After a coffee break they heard further talks on industrial relations and training, by Manpower Adviser W. P. Allen, C.B.E. and Sir John Benstead. In the following days they visited the new town of Basildon, and attended a sherry party at the London Mansion House. On the Saturday they returned by train to Oxford to rejoin the other groups.

The Duke of Edinburgh presided over the meeting in Oxford where each group reported back on the things they had seen. It became plain that men in the same groups had looked at the same things from different points of view, and the meetings at Oxford brought all these viewpoints together. There were reports of bad, or monotonous, conditions of work, but it emerged that human relationships counted for a great deal. Farmworkers, miners, dustmen and sewermen all expect dirty work to some extent and are prepared to put up with it, if they get the right leadership. A good leader will build good relationships which will produce good, honest work. Workers need to feel that they are part of a concern, whether it be factory, shop, office or farm. They need to feel that they are contributing to future prosperity and success, to be able to take a pride in their jobs. Prestige, status and promotion are to be aimed for; holidays and good pay matter. The values which emerged during the conference were to be fought for by the unions in future years, and Frank felt proud to have been there. Many refreshing and enlightening things were said during the conference, many friendships established, prejudices were removed and convictions deepened and strengthened. To Frank one lesson was uppermost. While conditions of work, such as pleasant surroundings, bright colours and modern sanitation, are important, they are not enough. Good human relationships cannot be bought with flower beds, glossy paint and fancy colour schemes. The main factor is good leadership, a willingness to consult with one another, a sense of purpose and challenge, and the rewards of promotion allowing real ability to show itself.

The conference ended with a summing up at Rhodes House. It was agreed to set up regional study groups in the U.K. to observe industrial relations in their areas and report back to a central committee in London which would arrange a weekend conference at two-year intervals. Frank was one of those elected to the committee, and for six years they held regular meetings two or three times a year at the Shell-Mex buildings overlooking the Thames. Weekend conferences were finally held at Horsley Towers, Sussex, Bognor Regis and other places, all of which proved successful.

1956 also saw the Suez Crisis, when Sir Anthony Eden involved Britain by taking military action against Egypt. Opinions as to the wisdom of his actions differed and much criticism was levelled against him, with cries of 'Eden must go!' Frank's eldest son, serving with the Royal Marine Commandos, was with the landing party, and assured his father that the troops were solidly behind Eden and that Nasser was on the run. Through pressure from the U.S.A., Britain withdrew its troops and Nasser blocked the shipping routes through the Suez Canal.

Chapter Fifteen

THE ETERNAL CITY

The year 1957 gave Frank his first chance to visit Rome, the eternal city, travelling by air as a member and Government adviser with the U.K. delegation headed by Earl St. Aldwyn to the United Nations' Food and Agricultural Organisation (F.A.O.) conference. The headquarters of the F.A.O. in Rome were opened in 1951 after a move from Washington. During his month-long stay at the Hotel Royal, Frank made friends from all parts of the world. This was the start of ten years of F.A.O. work as a Government adviser with many trips to Rome and other European cities. During this first visit he had the honour to be received in audience by Pope Pius XII at his summer residence outside the city. Outside were beggars on their knees and women selling violets, while inside the delegates met the head of the Roman Catholic Church, whose influence was tremendous all over the world. The Pope, recently recovered from a serious illness, looked very pale as he entered the room where the delegates were assembled. Seated upon his throne, attended by his Swiss Guards in their colourful and picturesque uniforms, he addressed them and gave his blessing to the work of the F.A.O. He then mingled with the guests for a while, chatting as medals were distributed to all as mementos of the visit. Frank's impression was that the Pope was a sick man, kind and affectionate, and carrying a heavy load of responsibility.

The long stay in Rome enabled Frank to explore the city, with its historical and Biblical connections. One Sunday, accepting an invitation from one of the permanent staff at the F.A.O. headquarters to be taken on a ride over the Italian Alps, Frank was surprised when picked up at noon to find that he was to travel in a low sports car. Away they went, out of Rome and down the Appian Way, past the place known as Quo Vadis where, according to legend, St. Peter had a vision of Christ and was persuaded to return to Rome and martyrdom. Frank was taken to visit the Ardeatine caves, where on 24 March, 1944, 335 Italians were massacred by the Nazis. They are commemorated by a mausoleum, and every year a march to the scene of the tragedy is held. As Frank stood outside the cave, blocked by a great boulder describing the massacre, he thought of Pope Pius XII and wondered if it was true that he refused to stop the slaughter for fear of upsetting the Vatican's good relations with the Nazis. Frank became friendly with Dr. Gordon Wright, Deputy Director General, of the F.A.O., and Sir Beresford Pearce of the Forestry Commission, both of whom lived in Rome. Through these two, Frank was able to visit many of the ruins, churches, museums and famous buildings in his ten years of visits to the eternal city. One Sunday morning he rose early and visited St. Peter's Cathedral, spending some four hours in this magnificent building. He saw the large numbers of pilgrims and worshippers and witnessed the long procession of cardinals and priests before the High Mass. Only those who have seen the High Mass with its huge choir and long drawn-out ceremonies at the altar can ever visualise the immensity of it all. As a Methodist, Frank found the spectacle something entirely new.

Enjoyable though the sight-seeing was, it was not the purpose of the visit. The F.A.O., (pronounced 'FOW'), founded in Quebec in 1945, following World War II, was born out of the idea of freedom from want and the necessity to improve efficiency in the production and distribution of food. There was also concern to raise levels of nutrition and standards of living, and to better the conditions of rural dwellers and expand rural agricultural economy in all nations. The first conference in Quebec, Canada, was attended by 45 nations, but, by the time Frank began his F.A.O. work, this number had grown to 126. The Rome headquarters was a large, imposing, modern building, one block of which was originally built by Mussolini as his Colonial Office. Here some 2,000 people were employed, mostly from Britain and America. The World Conference was held every two years, with delegations from many countries and observers from the various U.N. organisations and other international bodies. Between the biennial conferences, regional conferences were held in Rome and other cities within the regions. In spite of the size of the delegations, each country was allowed only one vote.

The World Conference began in the large Plenary Assembly Hall before splitting up into various commissions to study the various aspects of F.A.O. work, each commission having its own conference room fully equipped with the latest simultaneous translation system. This made it possible to hear an interpretation as the speaker made his speech, English, French and Esperanto being commonly used. Every morning the British delegation would meet at 8 a.m. at the hotel, where they would be joined by delegates from the Commonwealth to report on their commissions and receive instructions for the day. With only one vote per delegation, naturally there was much lobbying in order to try to obtain votes on the many matters to be decided by the plenary conference. It was very enjoyable, with regular social functions, luncheons and cocktail parties, with invitations coming from the various nations, but it was also very hard work, the delegates often meeting from 10 a.m. to 10 p.m., with a two-hour break for lunch from 1 p.m. to 3 p.m. in the large restaurant or adjoining special restaurants. Frank was keenly interested in the under-developed countries, having seen at first hand the miseries of the poverty-stricken people of China, India and Egypt. This was the main reason for his long connection with F.A.O., which was only terminated after ten years on medical advice due to heart trouble.

On his return Frank was kept busy with his work for the Union and various local government committees, including the Yorkshire Transport Users' Consultative Committee, of which he had been a member since its inception in 1952. The Committee was concerned with hearing objections to the proposed closure of some non-profitable rural lines. In 1958 Frank was appointed Justice of the Peace for the South Holderness Petty Sessions, being sworn in at the East Riding Quarter Sessions at Beverley in January. This honour brought him congratulations from a wide area. Over the years he found the work tremendously interesting and became Chairman of the Juvenile Bench and Deputy Chairman of the Bench, and served on the Crown Courts until 1976.

In the N.U.A.W. the case for a wages structure was still causing a great difference of opinion. The left-wing element was greatly opposed to any form of wages structure for agriculture, but the majority of far-seeing workers, including the East Riding members, felt that only a wages structure could eventually bring advancement and increased rates of pay for skilled workers and those with special responsibilities, as was the case in industry generally. The biennial conference in 1958 was held at Sandown, Isle of Wight, attended by about 200 delegates. The Union President, Edwin Gooch, M.P., was unable to attend through illness, so the senior member of the N.E.C., W. Case, presided. The usual demands for wage increases were to the fore, a resolution for a substantial increase being carried in place of a more moderate one for £9 per week. There was a heated discussion on the issue of a wages structure. The motion was strongly opposed by the left wing, who urged consultation to all branches before any decision was taken, with the matter being reported back to the 1960 conference. However, the motion for the N.E.C. to present a wages structure to the Central Agricultural Wages Board as early as possible was passed by a substantial majority. It is interesting to note at this point that the wages structure was not actually implemented until March, 1971. During conference week, delegates were taken on a tour of the beautiful Isle of Wight and the usual social functions were held.

In October, Frank attended the Labour Party Conference at Scarborough as one of the N.U.A.W. delegates, the agricultural debate being one of the highlights. The policy document, *Prosper the Plough*, and the Union's own document, *Health and Wealth under our Feet*, were discussed. The nationalisation of all land did not meet with the approval of many delegates. The Union felt that, while the nationalisation of farm land might be possible, it was not desirable to nationalise the lot — from large estates to the smallest privately-owned holding or back garden. The passing by Conference of *Prosper the Plough* meant that, before any schemes to nationalise the land were made, a pilot scheme should be set up to see how it could be administered and carried out.

Frank Robinson (left) and Hubert Luckett (right) after 21 years in the Union together.

Chapter Sixteen
FREEDOM FROM HUNGER

Frank was again re-elected to the N.E.C. in 1959. He attended the Winter School at Clacton, one of the speakers being John Anderson of the F.A.O. The value of these schools was immense, and Frank found the ones he attended at Oxford, Matlock and other places to be most helpful to him in his work. Rural housing was generally one of the subjects raised, and as a rural district councillor who served on the Housing Committee he took a major part in the debates. The President, the General Secretary of the T.& G.W.U., T. Heeley, and Frank formed a deputation to the Ministry of Agriculture to protest against the rejection of the Union's claim for a 44-hour week.

In June, Reg Bottini, Bill Case and Frank went on a study tour to Sweden to observe the wage structure and conditions of farm and forestry, on behalf of the European Productivity Agency in Paris. Frank took the opportunity to renew old acquaintances. The group travelled by air and stayed at the Airport Hotel, some twenty minutes by tube from Stockholm. Sweden is half as big again as Great Britain, and is largely a country of lakes and forests, the average being 50% arable and 50% forest, though in the northern areas forests predominate. The delegates spent some time in discussion with Swedish trade union officials, visited many Swedish farms, and had interviews at Runooskolan Trade Union School, Akersberga, with Forestry Commission officials. They spent some happy hours visiting farmworkers' cottages in the Orebro district, and had the pleasure of having tea and staying the night with an old friend, Alex Bloom of the Swedish farmworkers' union. Most of the Swedish farmworkers lived in tied cottages, and the rent was fixed according to whether the cottages were graded as first, second or third class. All the cottages had electricity, a good piped water supply, and modern furniture, many also being centrally-heated. The upper rents were double and triple the English rents, which had been set at 6s. per week. The wages structure allowed for fifteen specialist grades, such as farm foremen, farm mechanics, tractor drivers, mechanics, *etc.*, with rates up to 13% above the general farm rates. The 45-hour week was in operation, and general legislation in all industries forbade the working of overtime to a total of more than 200 hours in any one year. The only benefits payable from normal industrial protection were unemployment and funeral benefits. Accident benefit and sick pay came from the state, but free legal aid was given in all matters arising out of employment. Wages were fixed at a basic hourly rate of 4s. 9d. (English money). The visit had a very full programme, almost every moment being spent in travelling, meetings and visits, but everywhere they were received with generous hospitality. Billy Case was that year honoured by being awarded the M.B.E. for his many years' service to agriculture and local government in Wiltshire.

On his return to England, Frank paid a visit to the Land Settlement Association's chief holdings at Foxash, Essex. These holdings under the provisions of the Agriculture Act, 1947, went for preference to agricultural workers, and in 1957 there was a large demand for them. Estates of this type were to be found in thirteen counties, including Yorkshire.

During the year Sidney Dye, M.P., lost his life in a car accident, and at the subsequent by-election his seat was captured by Albert Hilton, one of the Union's Norfolk Organisers. In October there was another general election, with four of the Labour candidates being members of the N.U.A.W. — Edwin Gooch, Albert Hilton, Len Pike and John Stewart. The Conservatives again won the election, but two of the Union men, Edwin Gooch and Albert Hilton, won their seats, though Hilton's majority was reduced to only 78 votes.

The Lord Mayor's Show in London on 14 November had an agricultural theme, and the Union had a float, drawn by a tractor, showing a worker dressed in spraying equipment and a dairyman complete with milking unit, backed by a large photograph of a worker on a tractor. Much hard work went into the preparation of this float, which was only made possible by the commercial firms which provided the items of equipment.

At the end of November Frank again attended the F.A.O. Conference in Rome as a Government adviser. The work to save lives and provide for a decent level of nutrition for all the peoples of the world had become even more urgent. War, pestilence and famine were still taking a heavy toll of human life, with starvation being the biggest threat. Recent advances in medical science, supported by large scale public health measures, had gained many victories against epidemic and endemic diseases. The problems of feeding the world's population were growing, with hunger and want in many parts of the world, and the world population expected to double by the year 2000. Thus it was that the Director General of the F.A.O., B. R. Sen, appealed for a 'Free the World from Hunger' Campaign which he hoped would receive the support of all governments and non-government organisations connected with F.A.O., which would amount to a re-dedication of all that the F.A.O. Charter stood for.

At this conference, Frank's work centred mainly on the Technical

Committee dealing with nutrition. A great deal of work had been done in this area in collaboration with the World Health Organisation and U.N.I.C.E.F., but the problem arose of widening the scope of the work on the existing resources and personnel. At the time there was only one F.A.O. officer in that department, yet essential work was needed to gain knowledge of the types of food needed in certain areas. There was also a great need for more teaching on nutritional problems and further studies on processing and preserving food, and on the needs of young and growing people. As a Belgian delegate put it, what was needed was a world map of food and a world map of hunger. One of the major points of discussion was the sudden reduction in supplies of dried milk from the U.S.A. The milk had been distributed through U.N.I.C.E.F. and other agencies, and some 35,000,000 people in 62 countries had benefited. In view of the lack of protein-rich foods in many countries, this drop in supplies was a cause for major concern. The U.S.A. indicated that the drought in Europe had so affected their sales of milk that they had had to cut their supplies to U.N.I.C.E.F. by some 25%. They expected to be able to restore them by June, 1960. Frank was also able to attend meetings of the Animal Health Division, the health of the world's stock being of great importance. Anything done to reduce the death toll due to rinderpest and other diseases made a further contribution to the level of food production. Some 46 countries also gave their support to a world seed campaign designed to develop and use high quality seeds and varieties.

Following this conference, Frank attended an F.A.O. regional conference in Paris in the spring of 1960, on this occasion as a representative of the European Landworkers' Federation (E.L.F.) The discussions which followed covered many subjects such as rural sociology, mechanisation, housing and migration.

At the North and East Yorkshire annual conference of the N.U.A.W., the President presented Tom Williams, former Minister of Agriculture, with the Gold Badge, the Union's highest award. Tom Williams had been known in the House as 'Honest Tom' and was the only member who could claim to be an expert on both coal and farming. Farm safety came under discussion, especially the lifting of heavy weights. Regulations were made that the maximum weight of any load carried in a sack or bag unaided by a worker employed in agriculture should be 180 lbs. Implementation was delayed until July in order to allow for provisions to be made and the correct sacks to be supplied. Young persons under 18 were protected, it being an offence to employ a young person to lift, carry a load or move it, that was so heavy as to be likely to cause injury. Frank thought of his days as a strong lad of 17, carrying very heavy sacks on threshing day.

The Union's biennial conference was held in Chester Town Hall. In addition to the usual topics, the spread of nuclear weapons was discussed. A resolution was passed to urge the Government to cease the manufacture, testing, and stockpiling of nuclear weapons and to seek an international agreement for total disarmament. Further wage increases were gained by farm workers, a minimum of £9 per week to apply from 2 January, 1961. The introduction of a wages structure suffered long delays, as the N.F.U. members refused to commit themselves until they could discuss the matter with their county branch members.

At the Labour Party Conference at Scarborough in October, the anti-Gaitskell faction accused him of wanting to abandon nationalisation. Hugh Gaitskell vindicated himself and won the support of the majority of delegates in a fine speech in which he said that he had no intention of abandoning public ownership and accepting for all time the present frontiers of the public sector. He regarded public ownership not as an end in itself, but as a means, and not necessarily the only or most important one, to certain ends, such as full employment, greater equality and higher productivity.

Also in October, Frank again returned to Rome for a specially convened European Regional Conference of F.A.O. to discuss the main objectives for the 1961 conference and to further discuss the Freedom from Hunger Campaign. It was the first conference of its kind, and the Director General recapitulated the events leading to the convening of the conference and hoped that governments which had sent representatives would appreciate the value of it. Frank represented the E.L.F. and was able to speak, making the point that it would be wrong for governments to aim at reducing agricultural employment, even if increased mechanisation made it inevitable. Rather than farmers spending capital on purchasing expensive machinery which was only used for short periods of the year, it would be better for small units to work together and pool their resources. This point was supported by the Belgians and other delegates. Mr. Sen made an emphatic appeal for greater governmental participation in the Freedom from Hunger Campaign. So far, he said, the response had not been great, and he urged the governments to stimulate national interest and activities. Many governments had not shown the sense of urgency that was expected. So far, since the launch of the campaign in July, they had received some $300,000 but much more was needed, and he urged all governments and non-government organisations to support the campaign. During the discussions that followed, Frank was called upon to speak, expressing his concern at the mild response from governments. He pointed out that the work of the F.A.O. was not generally known, and suggested that radio and television should be used to publicise it. He suggested that a series should be made on the work of the F.A.O. and the need for the Freedom from Hunger Campaign.

In the New Year Honours for 1961, the General Secretary of the N.U.A.W., Harold Collinson, was awarded the C.B.E., the Chairman of the A.W.B., G. G. Honeymoon was knighted, and Tom Williams became a life peer. During 1961 the A.W.B. discussions were chiefly concerned with the proposed wages structure and the rates payable to the various skilled workers. A further 6s. per week was gained on basic wages. The Common Market talks caused division of opinion, with the Conservatives in favour, but the Labour Party adopting a 'wait and see' policy, unwilling to commit themselves until some of the many problems had been ironed out.

In November, Frank again attended the F.A.O. conference at its H.Q. in Rome. In his opening remarks, Mr. Sen paid tribute to the work of Dag Hammarskjold and referred to the Pope's encyclical which had mentioned the work of the F.A.O. in the fight against world poverty and hunger. It was the first time an organisation of this kind had been singled out in this way. Mr. Sen spoke of the increasing realisation that peace could not be secure while half the world's population was denied the chance of a tolerable existence. The leader of the U.K. delegation, Earl Waldegrave, urged that brave new ventures should not be entered into without careful preliminary planning and the assurance that people were available to carry out the work. In reference to Britain's Freedom from Hunger Campaign, he said that pledges of support in excess of £2 million had been received.

One of the highlights of the conference was the second MacDougall Memorial Lecture delivered by J. D. Rockefeller of the Rockefeller Foundation. In the MacDougall Memorial Lecture the speaker is given considerable latitude to choose his own topic, and does not necessarily express views which would be supported by the F.A.O. Mr. Rockefeller's main theme was the unchecked growth of world population which was exceeding the rate at which food production was increasing. He called upon the nations of the F.A.O. to face the facts and their implications, and to determine whether population stabilisation was necessary and feasible in their countries. The Director commented that, although the problem was of concern to all thinking people, there were many differences of approach, and he felt that the F.A.O. was primarily concerned with the increase of food production. It was proposed by the Canadian delegation that a World Food Aid Bank should be created. Millions of pounds worth of food surpluses, mainly from the U.S.A., were already being distributed on special terms to the hungry peoples, and the proposal was accepted.

Chapter Seventeen

HONOURS AND DEPARTURES

In the New Year Honours of 1962 Bert Hazell, the East Yorkshire District Organiser, received the C.B.E. in recognition of his seven years' service as Chairman of the East and West Riding Regional Board for Industry. As Vice-chairman of the Hull and East Riding Board of Industry, Frank had had the pleasure of serving under Bert's chairmanship at Leeds. Bert had previously been awarded the M.B.E. in 1946. Frank's Council activities and Union work continued unabated. Farmworkers were continuing to leave the land, there being some 19,000 fewer in 1962 than in the previous year. This meant more pressure for increased wages and the introduction of a wages structure, especially in the light of changing methods due to mechanisation and electrification. Up in Northumberland Frank had the pleasure of presenting Jack Short on his retirement with a set of pipes in appreciation of his 22 years as Chairman of the County Committee. He had been a great friend of Frank, who had spent many happy days at Jack's home in Chathill. The Union's biennial conference at Bournemouth brought the usual heated discussions on wages, tied cottages, farm accidents and the Common Market. Much concern was voiced on the number of fatal accidents occurring with tractors, 120 in the previous three years, half of them involving people between 16 and 19 years of age. As regards the Common Market, it was felt that obligations to the European Free Trade Association, the Commonwealth and British agriculture were stronger than the need to enter the E.E.C., and the Conference voted against joining at that time.

William Holmes, the grand old Norfolk pioneer of the Union, died in his 90th year. He had started work at the age of 12 for five shillings a week, and had been one of George Edwards' members when the Union was founded in 1906, and held the office of General Secretary from 1928 until 1945, when he retired. He was Union President from 1922 to 1928, and Frank had the joy of serving with him on the N.E.C. between 1942 and 1945, going with him to many conferences, addressing open air meetings and on occasions sharing a room with him. He was a kindly, fatherly, considerate man, hating snobbery, a great lover of the countryside, and highly respected by leading trade unionists and politicians of all parties. He was well-read, a lover of classical literature. In his day he had served under Keir Hardie, and been a member of the old Independent Labour Party.

The European Landworkers' Federation held its Congress in London in August, 1962, this being the first Congress since the I.L.F. had merged with I.F.P.A.W. Decorative banners of all 13 countries represented hung on the walls of the Cora Hotel. Frank was able to renew his friendship with old acquaintances from Austria, Belgium, Germany, Denmark, Italy, Holland, Norway and Sweden, and he had the pleasure of being one of the speakers to address the Congress. He had to return home early, however, as his wife was taken seriously ill in hospital in Hull. After a trying time she recovered, and Frank paid her a glowing tribute for all her help to him. Throughout his travels at home and abroad, she answered the many calls received at home in his absence. Mass rallies throughout the country found Frank addressing open air meetings at Newark, Retford and Morpeth, as well as attending the Labour Party Conference at Brighton. With him at Brighton was Charlie Chandler, an old N.E.C. member who had represented the Midlands for almost 30 years. He was a cheerful chap, and he and Frank were good friends, although they often differed in their views. During their free time at Brighton he took Frank and Hubert Luckett on several rides in his car. He left them at the weekend in cheerful spirits

F.A.O. in Rome. Frank Robinson in glasses, second from left. Sir Christopher Soames (later Lord Soames) front right.

77

saying, 'See you next week at the E.C.!' Unfortunately he died that weekend, aged 68. It was a big loss, not only to his many friends, but to the Union. At the end of 1962 Frank was again re-elected to the N.E.C., having completed 20 years of continuous service.

In 1963 Frank was appointed by the Ministry of Labour as Chairman of the Hull and District Employment Committee, replacing Philip Priestman who retired at the age of 70. Having served on the committee as a member for 17 years, Frank knew the importance of the post, especially with the large numbers of unemployed in the Hull area. It was a sad year for the Labour Party, as both Hugh Gaitskell, Leader of the Party, and Morgan Phillips, General Secretary, died in January, 1963. Frank had met them both on several occasions, and shared platforms with them, for both men had great interest in the N.U.A.W. Ted Calver was elected to the N.E.C. to replace Charlie Chandler. He and Frank soon became friends.

In November Frank again attended the F.A.O. Conference in Rome as an adviser to the British Government, under the leadership of Christopher Soames, at that time Minister of Agriculture. Discussions again took place on the Freedom from Hunger Campaign. Since it began in 1960 it had captured the hearts of many people, and most people had made some contribution. In Britain the Oxfam relief fund had been started, in which voluntary organisations were to sponsor the appeal in order to make a special contribution to the fund. A move by Ghana to exclude South Africa from the F.A.O. failed; though they obtained majority support, it was not the two-thirds required by the constitution.

Pope Pius had died in 1958 amidst great criticism concerning his part in the massacre of Italian partisans and his relationship with the Nazis. Pope John XXIII had unexpectedly been elected to replace him. Frank had the pleasure of being presented to Pope John on two occasions, while serving with the F.A.O. His admiration for this best-loved of popes was very great, and he was very grieved by his death in 1963. He was succeeded by Pope Paul VI, a man of high intellect, a diplomat and an ex-Minister of State. Frank was also received by Pope Paul in 1963. Afterwards, as they retraced their way down the 250 steps leading to St. Peter's Square, one of the cardinals, seeing Frank's disability, said, 'Come, let me take you down in the Pope's lift.' As they travelled down, he told Frank that his name was Robinson. As they laughed over the coincidence and chatted to each other, Frank learned that he had gone out from Lancashire to Africa as a missionary and had later been sent to the Vatican.

The close of 1963 will always be remembered for the assassination of President John F. Kennedy. The F.A.O. Conference was still in session, and, after the morning session the next day, when tributes were paid to the President, the work was ended for the day. Every delegate went out and bought a black tie, and on Sunday, 24 November, they attended a memorial service at St. Paul-Within-the-Walls, an American Episcopalian Church in

Rome, conducted by the Rector, Rev. Wilbur Charles Woodhams. A requiem mass was held in St. John's later, led by Cardinal Spillman, with admission by ticket only.

1964 opened with another great loss to the Union with the deaths of Hubert Luckett and Arthur Monks, both great Union stalwarts and personalities. Hubert and Frank had been very close friends, being nicknamed the E.C. Twins, having joined the N.E.C. together and having served for 22 years. Frank was with Hubert at the Winter School at Clacton, and they had retired to their rooms in great happiness, having shared a drink together. Next morning the chambermaid brought Frank's morning tea at 7 a.m. and told him the gentleman next door wanted him. He went to Hubert's room and, realising he was very ill, called the doctor, but before help could arrive Hubert, in the presence of Ted Calver whom Frank had called in, passed away. While the hotel guests had their breakfast, Frank stayed with Hubert while the police took the details, the doctor arrived and Hubert was taken to the rest room of a local undertaker. Hubert was 69 years of age, and had been Secretary of the Chislet Branch in Kent for 39 years, right up to his death. His loss to Frank could not be expressed in words. Arthur Monks was a retired Organiser, and during the war had been Labour Liaison Officer to the Ministry of Agriculture. He had served the Union well in the Spalding area of Lincolnshire.

In April, 1964, another Union stalwart, Josh McCage, from Rossington, West Yorkshire, passed away. He had, as a tribute to his 40 years of service to the Union, been made a life member only a week before his death. Frank had served with him on the N.E.C. for two years, but had known him since leaving the Army, having served with him on the Yorkshire County Committee and having stayed at his home while visiting the Rossington area as the N.E.C. representative.

The Union's biennial conference took place at Felixstowe, Suffolk. The widening gap between the wages of agricultural workers and those of other industries was causing great concern. Pressure was also applied to get the A.W.B. to set up the wages structure and it was suggested that T.U.C. help be enlisted. The five-day, 40-hour week was also advocated, and the tied cottage as usual came in for strong criticism. The matter of wages while sick was also discussed. Edwin Gooch was re-elected as President, with Albert Hilton as Vice-president.

In August, 1964 the Union was dealt another heavy blow with the death of President Edwin Gooch at the age of 75. His death marked the end of an era, for he was the last of the public-spirited men who, although never farmworkers, took up the challenge and marched with the early pioneers to support their fight for recognition. He had originally been a Norfolk blacksmith and had paved the way for the foundation of the Union in 1906. He was not only President of the Union from 1930 until his death, but also a life member of the National Union of Journalists, being the chief sub-editor of the *Norwich Mercury* for many years. He was an M.P. for many years, and became Chairman of the Labour Party. In 1956 he was able to preside over the Golden Jubilee celebrations of both the N.U.A.W. and the Labour Party, both having been formed in 1906. Frank worked with him for 22 years and went with him to many conferences. He was always ready to help anyone and never hesitated to tell anyone if he thought their views were not in the best interests of the Union. He had not intended to seek re-election to Parliament at the forthcoming general election. Many tributes poured in from home and abroad, but Frank always remembered him for his forthright honesty which won him respect throughout the country. A Methodist, he always had a clear and deep religious faith from which he gained his character and warmth.

1964 also brought the retirement of Fred Bond as Head of Finance at the Union's head office, having reached the age of 65. He was succeeded by his deputy, Bill Neate. The general election of 1964 saw Bert Hazell win the seat vacated by Edwin Gooch by a narrow majority of 53 votes, but Albert Hilton lost the South West Norfolk seat by 123 votes. After long negotiations with the Wages Board, the Union succeeded in obtaining an increase of 12s., bringing the national minimum to £10 2s. for a 45-hour week. Although a good increase, it was substantially less than the target of £12 for a 40 hour week.

1964-65 was the era of the 'Beeching Axe' when railways in rural areas throughout the country were being cut. Transport Users' Consultative Committees had been set up throughout the country, and Frank was one of the original members of the Yorkshire T.U.C.C. Protest meetings were held all over Yorkshire, and members of the Committee had to hear both the objections and the evidence of British Railways and later to give a decision. Many lines were saved from closure, including the Hull-Bridlington line after a hearing lasting two days, but the Hull-Withernsea, Hull-Hornsea, and Hull-York via Market Weighton lines were closed despite the strong objections of the Yorkshire T.U.C.C. It was a big blow for the people of Withernsea, Hornsea, Market Weighton and Pocklington. In spite of appeals to local M.P.s and the Prime Minister for the passenger services to be kept open, the last trains ran to Withernsea and Hornsea in 1964.

Chapter Eighteen

DIAMOND JUBILEE

Further honours came to the Union in 1965 when General Secretary Harold Collinson, C.B.E. was created a life peer in the New Year Honours List, taking the title of Lord Cheshunt after his place of residence. He had been elected as Chairman of the T.U.C. at the October, 1964, Conference. Frank was again re-elected to the National Executive Committee, and at home became Chairman of the recently set-up East Riding Agricultural Apprenticeship Committee. Bert Hazell, who had served the Union for 27 years as East Yorkshire Organiser, resigned to devote more time to his work as M.P. for North Norfolk, and was replaced by Colin Hands of Kent who had been serving as Recruiting Officer in Kent, Surrey and Sussex. Colin was well received in the East Riding, and Frank advised him not to try to be another Bert Hazell, but to be himself; the Yorkshire folk would soon get into his way of things if he spoke out. Another well-loved Union servant, Doris James, retired. She had been secretary to four General Secretaries, and was a valuable member of Head Office staff. Freddie Bond, the late Finance Officer, was also honoured in 1965, being awarded the M.B.E. for his outstanding work for the community in his capacity as J.P. and councillor for Bexley, Kent.

The Union lost another valuable servant with the sudden death of the head of the Legal Department, George Hook. He suddenly felt ill on his way home from Head Office and called in at the hotel where Frank was staying. Frank called an ambulance which rushed George to the University College Hospital. Frank went to the Angel underground station to meet George's wife who was coming to meet George before to going to a birthday party. He went with her in the taxi to the hospital and stayed with her. George died a few hours later. Frank attended the service at Streatham only a few weeks after attending his own brother's cremation at the same crematorium.

In spite of its grievous losses, the work of the Union continued. A claim by the N.E.C. for a 40-hour week instead of 45 was completely rejected by the A.W.B., which created strong resentment and criticism throughout the country. The Union had argued that, while only three industries in the country were on a 45-hour week, over 100 were on a 42-hour week. A special conference was called of all N.E.C.s of unions affiliated to the T.U.C. to discuss the Productivity, Prices and Incomes Policy. Over 1,200 delegates gathered in Westminster Central Hall to hear T.U.C. General Secretary George Woodcock outline the background of the negotiations. No one, he said, was claiming that the outcome was perfect. It was not a charter of rights, it did not provide a guarantee, but rather an opportunity. He pointed out that at one time it had been the exclusive interest of the trade union movement to look after the well-being of workers. Over the years, however, governments had come to share that responsibility, and the trade unions could not keep government at arm's length. The full debate brought many speeches for and against, but eventually on a card vote 6,649,000 votes were cast in favour of the policy and 1,811,000 against. The N.U.A.W. committee voted in favour of the report.

In July a conference of the International Federation of Plantation and Allied Workers (I.F.P.A.W.) was held in Amsterdam. Deep concern was expressed about world hunger and welcome given to the impetus of the F.A.O. and the Freedom from Hunger Campaign. Frank, speaking at the conference, told how the F.A.O. had already collected several million pounds, with Britain the highest contributor. He also spoke on the various projects of relief and technical aid carried out in under-developed countries

I.F.P.A.W., Amsterdam (1965). Frank Robinson, left hand, second row from front.

and the part being played by the British Government. He said that the chaotic state of the international supply of food made it essential to create a more rational system of food distribution throughout the world. It was suggested that a World Food Board be set up through the joint agencies of the Overseas Economic Development Council, the F.A.O. and the United Nations. Frank spoke of the U.N./F.A.O. World Food Programme, initiated in 1963, through which Britain had already sent several thousand tons of barley to the Middle East as part of its contribution. A World Food Board, if set up, must have the resources and executive powers that could really get to grips with the problem, for, in spite of all the aid given and efforts made in recent years, they had not even come close to a solution. Indeed, said Frank, they were as yet only scratching the surface and there was more poverty in India than 100 years ago. He drew attention to world poverty, malnutrition, disease and illiteracy, with the increase in population exerting a continual, remorseless pressure on resources. He said that developing countries must depend on their own exertions, but the wealthier nations must recognise their responsibility to help, both with financial aid and by providing advice and training facilities. He concluded with these words: 'It is a challenge we must all face, and, in facing the challenge, let us have patience in the task of building a better world and a fuller life for all mankind. It cannot be accomplished in a mere decade, nor even in a generation, but stirred by the greatness of the challenge, realising that food is more important than guns to win world peace, we can begin this noble work and, dedicated as we must be by patience, strength, hope and faith, in that spirit and with God's help we cannot fail.'

In October, after lengthy negotiations with the A.W.B., the Union succeeded in obtaining a rise of 8s. on the basic rate and one hour off the working week, bringing a wage of £10 10s. for a 44-hour week. After attending this meeting with the A.W.B., Frank travelled to Blackpool as the representative of the Holderness Rural District Council where, with the Public Health Officer, he attended the Public Health Conference. While there he was taken ill, collapsing at the *Black and White Minstrel Show* at the Winter Gardens. He awoke to find himself being attended to at the Victoria Hospital at about 1 a.m. He was very grateful to the Public Health Officer, Mr. Dyson, who did all that was necessary on Frank's behalf, collecting his luggage from the hotel and paying his bills. It was some months before Frank was able to resume active duties, missing the Labour Party Conference at Blackpool and another trip to Rome.

1966 was a momentous year in many ways. It was the Union's Diamond Jubilee, and the Agriculture Bill, with its prospects of a Training Board and the start of a wages structure negotiation, at long last made it a promising time. The new Rent Act, which came into operation in December, 1965, had an immediate effect on tied cottages, ensuring some protection from eviction for farm workers. The early months of 1966 also saw Frank return to his duties on the council and local committees. He also attended District dinners at Hull and York and took part in the Winter School at Clacton. The general election saw Bert Hazell re-elected for North Norfolk with a majority of only 737. The entry into Europe caused much controversy, but the Union was not opposed to Britain joining 'The Six' as long as adequate means were provided to safeguard the interests of British agriculture, the Commonwealth and E.F.T.A. In fact it was believed that the E.F.T.A. countries all joining the E.E.C. would be of benefit to them all.

In May Frank attended the Union's Diamond Jubilee Conference at Weston-super-Mare in Somerset. Having visited Somerset many times before while campaigning with D.O. Jack Humphreys, he was pleased to meet again with old friends and to take the opportunity to travel through the Cheddar Gorge and visit the place where Augustus Toplady composed the well-loved hymn *Rock of Ages* while sheltering from a heavy rain storm. The conference was held in the Town Hall, and during the week they were guests of the Mayor, Alderman F. Boyd, at a reception at the Winter Gardens Pavilion. As was the custom, the Somerset County Committee laid on a splendid dinner and concert to follow, after which Frank was presented with the Union's Gold Badge by the General Secretary, Lord Cheshunt, the highest Union award one can receive. At one of the rallies during the week to celebrate the Diamond Jubilee, one of the guest speakers was Anthony Wedgwood Benn, at that time Postmaster General. Bert Hazell was elected as President of the Union, and the usual conference matters were dealt with, including wages.

Another great rally to celebrate the Diamond Jubilee took place at Epworth, Lincolnshire, the birthplace of John and Charles Wesley, the founders of Methodism. On the Sunday afternoon a service was held in Epworth Parish Church, conducted by the Rev. W. Harvey. In the evening, at another service, Frank, as a Methodist, gave the address. Further rallies were held at Yarmouth and, of course, Tolpuddle. At Patrington they held a special event with Reg Bottini from Head Office presenting Silver Badges to 30 of the members.

At Brighton, at a special dinner during Labour Party Conference week, Frank was presented with the T.U.C. Silver Badge, an acknowledgement of his devoted work for his union.

Chapter Nineteen

NEW YEAR HONOUR

On New Year's Eve, 1966, Frank sat up all night with his next-door neighbour, Sydney Harrison, who passed away at 8 a.m. on New Year's Day at the age of 89. He was a good musician and had actually played the organ at St. Patrick's Church, Patrington, at the age of 12 years. In the morning paper, among the New Year Honours, appeared the name of Francis Robinson, awarded the O.B.E. This was a great honour, not only for him personally, but also for all the people and organisations that Frank had served with over the years. It was an award not only for his long service in the trade union movement, but also for his work with the F.A.O. and on the many agricultural committees and in local government.

The Investiture at Buckingham Palace was a great day for Frank, and for his wife Mona and his daughter Patricia, who were able to sit in the great ball-room with the other relatives whose family members were receiving honours that day. For something like two hours they watched the ceremony, while the Guards' String Orchestra played quietly in the background, with the Queen, Lord Chamberlain and other officials on the platform at the front. Later, Frank, Mona and Patricia went to the House of Commons where they were met by Bert Hazell, M.P., and taken to lunch in the House. Afterwards they went to the Public Gallery to listen to some debates. In the evening they went to the Adelphi Theatre to see *Charlie Girl*. They spent a few days together at the hotel in London before returning home.

There was anger and dismay in the Union when the Government insisted that the wage increase had to be ratified by the Prices and Incomes Board, but, after hearing the farmworkers' case, the increase was allowed. Taking into consideration the low wages paid in agriculture, the T.U.C. allowed another pay claim immediately, and after a 7-hour marathon meeting a further rise of 15s. was allowed, to come into operation in February, 1968. Bob Stanley, the Durham and Northumberland Organiser, who had reached the age of 65 three years earlier, had not been in good health since a car crash and decided to retire in 1967. His place was taken by Terry Hammond, from Beeford, East Yorkshire, who had gained a T.U.C. scholarship and degree at Hull University.

Zachariah Bemrose, Frank's valuable and stalwart friend, died in 1967. Frank had been born in the same row of cottages as Zach, and had lived next door to him during his first seven years of married life. They had worked together on the farm, and for days Frank used to stand in the first 'pick-hole' at harvest time while Zach built his high corn pikes that were the envy of other stackers for miles around. In his early days as a trade unionist, Zach was victimised and out of work for his principles, but gained employment as a part-time gardener and found himself better off than when working on the farm. His skill and ability showed in his work, however, and he was soon back on the farm with much higher wages than the usual rates. In Union meetings he was a passionate orator, and on one occasion his enthusiasm got the better of him and, banging his fist on the table, he sent it crashing from the platform onto the packed benches below. Always spick and span, with a smart pointed moustache, he was a local preacher, choir master and soloist with a firm faith in God and a clear sense of duty to help the working classes. His honesty and integrity won him the respect of the farmers who had once despised his principles, and in later years he served on the Parish Council. During a period when Frank was seriously ill, Zach was his greatest friend, giving ungrudging practical help where it was most needed.

The trade union movement and Labour Party suffered another sad loss in 1967 with the death of 'Honest Tom' Williams, who had been Minister of Agriculture from 1945 to 1951. In steering the 1947 Agriculture Act through Parliament he had made one of the biggest single contributions to the success and prosperity of British agriculture. He was well known to Frank, having had close links with Patrington N.U.A.W.

In November 1967 Frank was able to attend the F.A.O. Conference in Rome once more. He was pleased to find some improvement in world food production and greater fairness in distribution between rich and poor countries. Yet with 60 million new mouths to feed every year, due to the ever-increasing population, it was a sobering thought that there were more under-nourished people in the world than ever before. The retiring Director General, Dr. Sen, received a standing ovation as an accolade for his outstanding work over the last eleven years, and was presented with a suitably-inscribed parchment. As he stepped down to be replaced by A.H. Boerma, Dr. Sen said, 'I have seen enough of poverty, misery, starvation and death to feel that the world community must be roused to the appalling conditions which exist in some parts of the world. My prayer is that one day the world will be free from hunger.' He and his wife were given another standing ovation as they left the hall.

During the year Frank went to Northumberland to help Terence Hammond and was able to spend time with Bob Stanley at a dinner at the Tankerville Arms, Wooler. At home Frank was still keenly interested in Council work and became Vice-Chairman of the Holderness Rural District

Council after serving as Chairman of the Health and Housing Committee for three years.

The year 1968 brought with it many joys, for at the N.U.A.W. conference at Aberystwyth Frank was able to meet his niece who had been one of the bridesmaids at his wedding back in 1931. Married to an R.A.F. lad during the war, Jean and her husband lived with their daughter Janet at Llanbadarn Fawr, Aberystwyth. Frank was able to visit them, invite them to dinner at the hotel, and spend a joyful weekend in that famous beauty spot around Devil's Bridge and the Vale of Rheidol with its narrow-gauge railway. At this conference the Union changed its name. Delegates had pressed strongly for the inclusion of allied workers, as it had been evident for many years that the labour force in agriculture was declining while the allied industries were increasing. The Union was to be known as the National Union of Agricultural and Allied Workers (N.U.A.A.W.), which was considered more fitting to the modern membership. A target of £16 was agreed for the new wage demand, farm safety was again discussed, and the Labour Government was criticized for its failure to implement its pledge to abolish the tied cottage. 1968 was the centenary year of the T.U.C., and processions took place in many large towns. The Union had its own float showing that agriculture was still Britain's biggest industry. To Frank, one of the most memorable events was the T.U.C. Centenary Banquet at the Guildhall in London on 5 June when Her Majesty the Queen was guest of honour for the evening. The Centenary reminded the country of the radical social changes that had taken place in one hundred years — how the T.U.C. had developed from a small debating society into a national institution; how it had helped to prohibit the gross abuses of man's labour; how it had contributed to a new society with better social security, health and education services for all.

At long last there was hope that a wages structure for farm workers would be agreed by the A.W.B., with the opportunity for skills to allow a better standard of living. In the Holderness area the Union mourned the death of Jack Bird at the age of 88 years. He was a pioneer member of the Union who for many years had been the Chairman of the Ottringham branch and who was the holder of the Union's long service badge. Although he had had both legs amputated at the age of 80, he remained cheerful and enjoyed his eventide days in a council bungalow at Patrington.

Successful Union meetings were held during the year in Cumberland and Westmorland, and in the Wooler area of Northumberland. The Patrington branch celebrated its Golden Jubilee with a Jubilee Dinner attended by the President, Bert Hazell, and his wife, the District Organiser, Colin Hands, with his spouse, several long service members, and the Rev. Brierly, Methodist Minister, and his wife. John Drewery was the only member present who had joined the branch at its formation in 1918, and was a special guest at the top table.

In November more than 2,000 members from all parts of England and Wales converged on London to take part in the biggest demonstration by farm workers in the capital since the war. It was one of the most colourful rallies London had seen for some years. Banners in splendid array adorned the procession and vast numbers of posters and placards proclaimed the main points of the farm workers' claim of £16 for a 40-hour week. The procession was led by the Manchester Post Office Engeering Workers' Union Band, dressed in smart blue uniforms.

Jim Paull and Billy Case decided not to seek re-election to the Executive Committee. Between them they had some 85 years of Union membership. Billy served on the A.W.B. with Frank and they spent many happy times together in Wiltshire where Billy farmed a smallholding at Bowerchalk. He had won the T.U.C. Gold Badge and was awarded the M.B.E. He was a Methodist local preacher and an alderman on the County Council. Jim, a road foreman, was obliged to retire through ill health. He was jovial and warm-hearted, but a stickler for truth and principle. Before the end of the year another N.E.C. member had to retire, Bert Leader of Norfolk. He was an agricultural blacksmith by trade, but unfortunately lost the sight of one eye. Another great loss was the death of Freddie Bond, late Finance Officer, who had retired in 1964. He had served as a J.P. at Bexley, Kent, long after his retirement. After long hours of negotiation on wages, the Union was only able to obtain a 17 shilling increase, bringing the basic minimum to £12 8s. per week. In the N.E.C. elections, Frank was again re-elected, now being the Senior E.C. member, having served 26 years.

In November, 1968, Frank again travelled to the Dutch Landworkers' Conference at Utrecht on the River Rhine. While there he was able to visit the Delta Project which had been started after the terrible floods of 1953 which had killed some 1,800 people and rendered another 70,000 homeless. The main object of the project was to strengthen the coast and dykes and to combat the salination of the land and increase agricultural production. Frank was very impressed by the modern technology and engineering skills and was interested to compare the Dutch landworkers' problems with the British situation. He found that, although they were paid slightly more, the cost of living was higher, and on the whole their problems were very similar.

Chapter Twenty

TIME TO SAY GOODBYE

Early in 1969 the Union received a shock when it was learned that the proposed increase of 17 shillings in the minimum wage, which had been confirmed in November, 1968, was likely to be frozen by the Government. The Union's reaction was strong, as it was considered an unwarranted and unnecessary intervention by the Department of Employment and Productivity, whose Minister was Barbara Castle. Consequently a delegation from the Executive Committee, which included Frank, met the D.E.P. and forcefully expressed the Union's feelings, with the result that the Government withdrew its original proposals to allow only 10 shillings of the award and refer the remainder to the Prices and Incomes Board, and decided instead to refer the full proposal to the P.I.B. After much discussion the P.I.B. decided that, although the farmworkers' award was above the allowed 3½%, and thus could not be formally approved by the Board, they did suggest to the Minister that an exception be made in this case. On 30 January the Minister announced in the House of Commons that, in the light of the report, the Government did not propose to delay the implementation of the award. Also, at long last, the A.W.B. agreed on many points of the wages structure and on some sort of payment while sick. The Union decided to complete the wages structure and then press strongly for a statutory sick scheme.

Frank was kept busy with Union rallies in Driffield and Northumberland, as well as his Council work and other duties at home. Although never a fully accredited local preacher, he was designated a 'helper' and called upon to conduct worship and preach in the local Methodist circuit. There were also times of sadness and loss. The death occurred of Steve Wilson, one of the first members of the Tholthorpe, North Yorkshire, Branch of the Union, which had been opened by Frank in 1951. Another Union member, Bob Clarke of Norfolk, was elected to the N.E.C., but died before taking his seat. In October Harold Collinson retired as General Secretary in order to take up the post as Chairman of the Supplementary Benefits Commission. Frank had often stayed at his home, and was most disappointed that he was leaving, but he knew that the great experience he had gained would be put to full use in his new post. At the end of 1969 Dan Piggot, another of Frank's colleagues on the E.C., died in Manor House Hospital. He had been a keen Salvation Army man, was Secretary of the King's Lynn Divisional Labour Party, had many other interests, and was a keen pigeon fancier. He owned a smallholding where he grew strawberries, and each year the N.E.C. were treated to a strawberry tea at Head Office. Aged 72 at his death, he had led a full and active life, but had fallen ill shortly after returning home from the T.U.C. at Portsmouth. He had been elected to the N.E.C. in 1953, and Frank had served with him for the whole of those 16 years. Shortly afterwards, Frank too was taken ill at home, and was ordered by the heart specialist to take things easy. This meant that he missed the Northumberland County Conference and rally, an occasion to which he had looked forward as he could spend time with the Tynesiders whose interests he had served since 1942.

Reg Bottini succeeded Harold Collinson as General Secretary, which meant that Frank had served on the National Executive under four General Secretaries during his 28 years. He hoped to be able to serve for another two years, thus equalling the record of 30 years set by Billy Case of Wiltshire, but it was not to be. The heart specialist at Kingston General Hospital, Hull, told Frank plainly that if he did not stop chasing all over the country he would kill himself. Thus, at the end of 1970 Frank regretfully decided not to seek re-election to the N.E.C. He could, however, feel that he had retired in a year of success, for it was in 1970 that the statutory wage structure was implemented, which meant that in addition to the basic minimum of £13 3s. 0d. per week, skilled workers were able to receive 10%, 20% and 30% plus rates to bring wages without overtime as high as £17 2s. 0d.

Apart from his retirement, 1970 brought other sadness. The death occurred of Bob Stanley, who had retired as the Northumberland D.O. in 1967 due to ill health. Bert Huson of Norfolk, who had served on the N.E.C. for 12 years, also died at the age of 73 years. Bob Allcorn, the D.O. for Hampshire, also died, and at the end of the year Alf Pannell, a Union pioneer who had served on the N.E.C. until his retirement in 1958, died in his 90th year. Denis Hodson, the Assistant General Secretary, resigned in order to accept a post in Geneva as Assistant General Secretary with I.F.P.A.W.

As Frank looked back on his 28 years with the N.E.C. he recalled the many lasting friendships, the times when his duties had taken him abroad to all parts of Europe, and the many honours, including the T.U.C. Diploma for Special Organising Services, the T.U.C. Silver Badge, the Union's Gold Badge and the investiture of the O.B.E. by Her Majesty the Queen. He also acknowledged that without the loyalty, patience and support he received from his wife, often left alone with the family, he could never have achieved so much. The retirement also entailed severing

Frank Robinson as Chairman of Holderness Borough Council c.1971, with wife, Mona.

Mayor of Holderness, Councillor Tom Graham, presents the scroll to Frank as he is made an Honorary Freeman of the Borough of Holderness (1988).

connections with other organisations. Frank received letters from the members of the A.W.B., and also from the N.F.U., the F.A.O., civil servants in the Government and permanent officials in Rome. One of the simplest, yet one of the greatest compliments made on his retirement was by Stan Hayward, Editor of *The Landworker*, who wrote: 'As to our Union's future — one of its architects is Frank Robinson.'

Frank retained his Union and agricultural interests at home, and continued to serve on many committees for some years, being Chairman of the Agricultural Apprenticeship Committee for a long period. He was also determined to retain his great interest in local government as long as his health allowed. He had been one of the three councillors elected to serve his native town of Patrington since 1946. After reorganisation in 1974, only two councillors represented the ward which includes Patrington, Sunk Island and Hollym, with only one representative on the Humberside County Council for the area from Spurn to Burstwick, with the villages in between.

During his many years as a councillor, Frank found many matters dear to his heart, especially in regard to housing, health and environmental issues. He saw the number of council houses in Holderness rise from 230 before the war to some 1,500 by the seventies. During his term of office on the Holderness District Council he was Vice-chairman of the Health Committee 1961-64, Chairman 1964-67, Vice-chairman of the Council 1967-70, and Chairman 1970-72. In the interim period before to the 1974 reorganisation he was Chairman of the Steering Committee, and since, as a member of the Holderness Borough Council, has served as Chairman of the Health and Environment Committee. He also served on the Playing Fields Committee, retaining a great interest in sport, and from 1963 was Chairman of the Hull and District Employment Committee, until it became the Manpower Services Commission. He also continued his work as a magistrate, being Chairman of the Magistrates' Juvenile Bench, always endeavouring to treat the juveniles as a father would treat his own children.

Frank had always shown a keen interest in the history and traditions of his home village, and in retirement found the time to write a book, *Patrington — the Queen's Town: old customs and characters,* which was published by Lunns of Withernsea. (The title refers to St. Patrick's Church, which is called the Queen of Holderness.)

Frank was also a member of the Beverley and Holderness Branch of the Yorkshire Parish Councils Association and became its Chairman in 1963. After reorganisation in 1974 he became Chairman of the Holderness District Association. He stepped down from this office on 25 May, 1988, after 25 years as Chairman. In paying tribute to Frank's qualities, Albert Rimington, Secretary of the Humberside Association said: 'This is an incredible record of local government service which I have not heard of before — and he is still going strong!' Roy Garbutt of Bilton said that Frank had been a friend and adviser to all who were interested in local government and village life. He had been a member of the Holderness Council for 42 years, and of Patrington Parish Council for the same period. Frank, still serving as a Councillor at the age of 84, was given a standing ovation. At a special meeting of Holderness Borough Council held on 5 July, 1988, it was 'Resolved unanimously that Councillor Francis Robinson, O.B.E., J.P., be, and is hereby admitted to be an Honorary Freeman of the Borough of Holderness in recognition of his eminent services to the Borough Council and its constituent authorities as Councillor and of his untiring efforts to improve the image of the area and the quality of life of its inhabitants.'

The presentation was made on Monday, 10 October, 1988, which was Frank's eighty-fifth birthday. Councillors Richardson and Gledhill spoke in praise of Frank's lifetime of service, and Robin Taylor, Director of Development for Holderness, referred to Frank's inability to bear a grudge. 'We can disagree fundamentally about work,' he said, 'but he will come to me after a meeting and shake my hand.' Mayor of Holderness, Councillor Tom Graham, then presented Frank with the magnificent embossed scroll and a medal. In receiving the honour, Frank said that he had only one regret — that his 'Mam and Dad' could not be there; they would have been very proud. He concluded his speech by reminding the assembled company that in all we do we are members of the community, with all the responsibilities and privileges attached, and that councillors and officials must show tolerance and understanding in their dealings with their fellow-citizens.

The grant of an Honorary Freedom is a means of recognising the contributions made by someone who has proved to be a person of distinction and who has rendered eminent service to the authority and the community. It is a way in which the community can say thank you for a lifetime of service. Never has such an honour been more richly deserved than in the case of Frank Robinson, who, in spite of his travels around the world, remains the local lad from Patrington.

ABBREVIATIONS

A.W.B.	Agricultural Wages Board
C.Q.M.S.	Company Quarter-Master Sergeant
d.	(old) pence — before decimalisation, 12d. = 1 shilling = 5p
D.E.P.	Department of Employment and Productivity
D.O.	District Officer
D.O.R.A.	Defence of the Realm Act
E.C.	Executive Committee
E.E.C.	European Economic Community (Common Market)
E.F.T.A.	European Free Trade Association
E.L.F.	European Landworkers' Federation
F.A.O	Food and Agricultural Organisation of the United Nations
I.C.F.T.U.	International Confederation of Free Trade Unions
I.F.P.A.W.	International Federation of Plantation and Allied Workers
I.L.F.	International Landworkers' Federation
I.L.O.	International Labour Organisation
N.C.B.	National Coal Board
N.C.O.	Non-commissioned Officer
N.E.C.	National Executive Committee
N.F.U.	National Farmers' Union
N.H.S.	National Health Service
N.U.A.A.W.	National Union of Agricultural and Allied Workers
N.U.A.W.	National Union of Agricultural Workers
P.I.B.	Prices and Incomes Board
R.A.M.C.	Royal Army Medical Corps
R.S.M.	Regimental Sergeant Major
s.	shillings — before decimalisation, 20s. = £1
T.&G.W.U.	Transport & General Workers' Union
T.U.C.	Trades Union Congress
T.U.C.C.	Transport Users' Consultative Committee
U.N.	United Nations
UNICEF	United Nations' Children's Fund
W.A.E.C.	War Agricultural Executive Committee
W.F.T.U.	World Federation of Trade Unions
W.L.A.	Women's Land Army